Designs
for Self-Instruction

Designs
for Self-Instruction

Principles, Processes, and Issues
in Developing Self-Directed Learning

Johanna L. Keirns
San Jose State University

Allyn and Bacon
Boston · London · Toronto · Sydney · Tokyo · Singapore

For GHK

Table of Contents

Preface

Chapter One: Introduction 1

  What is "Self-Directed Learning?" 1

  Learning and Instruction 2

    Instruction: An implied contract 5

  What is the nature of self-instruction? 7

    Situations for self-instruction 7

    Principles of self-instruction 9

    Content for self-instruction:Domains of learning 11

    Kinds of content 14

  Expository/inquiry delivery styles 17

  Summary 18

  References and further reading 20

Chapter Two: Expository Self-Instruction—The Good Tutorial 23

  Historical background 25

  Programmed instruction 27

    Linear programs 27

    Branching programs 29

    Computer programs 30

  Designing Expository Instruction: Fundamental considerations 32

    Content and learners 32

    Process 33

  Establishing the implied contract 35

  Objectives: Real intent, indicators 36

    Audience 37

    Behavior: overt/covert 37

    Near or far transfer 39

    Conditions and degree 41

The planning pyramid   41
Fulfilling the implied contract   44
    Assessing attainment   44
    Criterion questions   46
Developing expository self-instruction:
Presenting information   49
    Content analysis   49
    Assuring active responding: Today's
    small steps   50
        Considerations for format   57
        Immediate feedback   61
        Sequencing   62
        Spiral learning   64
Guidance and practice   65
    Prompting   66
Representing the design plan   68
    Flowcharts   68
    Scripting   70
    Story boarding   71
"Student testing:" Formative evaluation   72
Summary   75
A Look ahead   76
References and further reading   77

Chapter Three: Inquiry- Based Self-
Instruction   79
    Theoretical background   80
        Away from behaviorism   80
        Schema theory   82
    Phases of experiential learning   83
    Formats for experiential learning   85
    Design considerations for inquiry-based
    instruction   87
        Content   88
        Learners   89
    Variations on the implied contract   90
        Establishing learning goals   90
        Evaluating outcomes   91

Planning experiential instruction: A model   94

    Selecting competencies   95

    Determining contexts   96

    Examining pre-requisite skills   98

Developing inquiry-based instruction   99

    Applying the principles of self-instruction to simulations   100

    Creating a global scenario   101

    Anchoring tasks   105

    Scaffolding   109

    Levels   109

    Help interactions   110

    Developing situations for interactions   112

    Reflective assessment points   114

    Keeping track of choices   116

Experiential learning and debriefing   118

Representing design/development work   119

    Flow chart variations   119

    Scripting   122

    Story boarding   123

Student testing of the material   124

Summary   124

A look ahead   125

References and further reading   127

Chapter Four: Issues In Self-Instruction And Self-Directed Learning   131

    Affective issues: Motivation, learning styles, interest   131

        Motivation   132

        Keller's ARCS model   133

        Attribution research   137

        Androgogy and pedagogy   140

        Engagement and games   142

Learning style variations and preferences 145
Interest 149
Metacognition 151
  Meta-cognitive skills 152
Summary 155
A look ahead 155
References and further reading 156

Chapter Five: Self-Directed Learning, A Final Look 159
Self-directed learning in collaborative settings 160
  Designing learning experiences 160
  Small group learning settings 161
Co-design as a concept for today 163
  Information management and co-design 165
Self-directed learning as a philosophy of education 167
Summary 169
References and further reading 170

Index 173

Preface

What to look for in this book

As you read this book, remember that in every way, the design of self-instruction is a special case of the broader discipline of Instructional Design. This book assumes that readers have a basic familiarity with the process of needs analysis, which includes careful investigation of proposed instructional settings to see whether instruction is in fact the best means to deal with the perceived knowledge or performance gap. (There are numerous excellent references for the instructional design process in general and for needs analysis in particular: a selection is given at the end of the introductory section.)

Sometimes improvement of a performance problem does *not* require people to learn something, but merely to have immediate access to information about how to proceed in a task. Because "performance support systems," particularly electronic aids, are often similar in form to self-instruction, particularly computer-based instruction, it is easy to confuse their purpose. Designing a good "job aid"or "electronic performance support system" is different from designing good self-instruction. This difference should be considered at the very outset of a design process. Throughout this book we are building on the assumption that learning is the intended result of the development of interactions with information which you will explore in these pages.

This book considers two broad approaches to the design and development of self-instruction and addresses design considerations essential for current delivery systems including multimedia, hypertext, and web-based delivery; but intentionally avoids specific recommendations for any particular delivery format. "Self-instruction" can be produced in many media, and "self-directed learning" is a concept independent of format, with many related issues calling for the designer's concern. Indeed, we are finding effective learning experiences combining more than one approach being developed throughout the community of Instructional Design professionals.

We can in these pages explore together some of the principles, processes and issues to be considered in the course of producing Designs for Self-Instruction which will facilitate learning for the diverse populations of learners with whom we work.

Acknowledgments

I would like to thank the reviewers who provided useful comments on early drafts of the manuscript.

James Lockard, Northern Illinois University
Stephen W. Harmon, Georgia State University
Terry L. Holcomb, University of North Texas
Marianne Handler, National-Louis University

Chapter One: Introduction

What is "Self-Directed Learning?"

The term "self-directed learning" may be understood in several ways. As a methodology for instruction, self-directed learning ordinarily refers to a learning situation in which an individual student or trainee works with instructional materials on his or her own time, without direct supervision or guidance from either instructor or fellow students. The format for such individual study materials may range widely, from print materials through audio tapes to interactive video, both in school and industry settings. This use of the term will be considered throughout this work, and the many implications of this view of "self-directed learning" will be discussed, as it relates to both theory and practice.

Theoretical investigations of "self-directed learning" or "self-regulated learning" in recent years have focused on meta-cognition, the skills and abilities which individuals employ to guide their cognitive experiences in learning situations. The use of the term in this sense will also be considered at length, as it clearly applies very directly to the situational uses described above.

A final use of the term "self-directed learning" carries a connotation of a philosophy of education, the viewpoint of educators who consider that the role of teachers should be to guide and facilitate the learning experiences of students, but that the learners themselves must be seen to be the actual directors of their learning. This viewpoint will also be considered in these pages.

Indeed, the three understandings named above may intersect very fruitfully in the design of contemporary instruction for a wide range of learners and settings, each definition illuminating the application of the others to maximize the development of successful learning materials and experiences for self-directed learning.

Learning and Instruction: Presenting Information vs. Providing Instruction

Daily life presents all of us with the constant necessity of dealing with bodies of information of many kinds. The news media, our work situations, our recreational choices, the conduct of our basic business affairs, all place us in the midst of interacting with quantities of

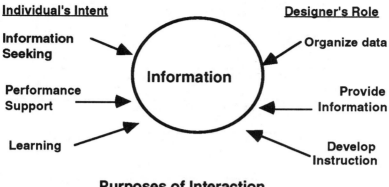

Purposes of Interaction

information in a variety of formats and for varying purposes, as the figure indicates.

Distinction needs to be made between the various purposes for an individual's interaction with a source of information, because these purposes affect the designer's role. People work with information with many different outcomes in mind, only one of which is *learning*. My students have identified numerous examples of such information sources and interactions, among them the following: an information kiosk at the airport; help screens in software programs; audio tapes for learning a language; an "Analyze your handwriting" booklet, instructions on how to take your own blood pressure with a kit; instructions for assembling or connecting equipment; ATM and self-service gasoline pump directions; a home pregnancy test kit; the DMV booklet for the driver's license test; instructions for programming your VCR.

•An information kiosk at the airport	
•Help screens in software programs	
•Audio tapes for learning a language	
•"Analyze your handwriting" booklet	
•Instructions on"How to take your own blood pressure" with a home-use blood pressure kit	
•Instructions for assembling or connecting equipment	
•ATM and self-service gasoline pump directions	
•Home pregnancy test kit	
•The DMV booklet for the driver's license test	
•Instructions for programming your VCR	

ACTIVITY

Before going further, consider which of these examples include "learning" as an outcome.

You probably selected the audio tapes and the DMV booklet as pretty clear examples of interaction with the intent of learning something as the outcome. The information kiosk, software help screens, medical kits and the VCR instructions may also imply "learning" as an outcome, but that outcome is much less the direct intent and purpose of the information presented. These examples, and the always-present directions at the ATM and gas pump, fall into the category of "job aid;" information presented for use at a particular point in time with no necessity that the information be stored for later recall. An interesting effect of repeated use of such job aids as help screens, instructions for taking one's blood pressure, and ATM directions is that learning *may* occur, and often does, in the sense that the user no longer needs to refer to the instructions with each use. (VCR programming instructions seem to present an exception to this observation in most people's experience.)

Instruction: An implied contract

When learning *may* occur, do we have a "self-directed learning" or "self-instructional" situation? I do not think so. Learning as an outcome for "self-instruction" is a necessary but not sufficient condition. Instruction, self-directed or otherwise, has further implications. *M. David Merrill (1990) poses the salient question: "What is it that instruction does to information that makes it different, that facilitates learning?" The following two aspects need to be present to make a learning opportunity represent an instructional setting:

First: Learning must be the *intended* outcome of the interaction with the information. The provider and the user of the information must both expect a change in the knowledge or skills of the user as a result of the interaction. When the nature of this change is stated, whether

*Used with permission of the author.

broadly or quite specifically, a sort of implied contract is established at the outset between the learner and the designer of the instructional experience.

Second: The learner's new knowledge or skill must be *demonstrated and evaluated against a desired standard* to fulfill the contract. In self-directed learning situations, this aspect is especially important, because the learner needs and expect to know the results of his own efforts.. The instruction must assure as far as possible all the necessary opportunities and assistance for the learner to reach the desired standard: the learner must invest the necessary effort and persistence to make opportunities and assistance bear the desired fruit, and he must perceive that he has acquired the potential ability to apply the new knowledge or skill successfully. It is the two-way interaction between learner and designer through the materials and setting for instruction which provides these opportunities and gives rise to this necessary feedback.

Thus, both *intent and evaluation* must be present in a learning situation for it to qualify as an instructional situation.

Consider the earlier examples once more: do all your original choices of learning outcomes match this definition?

The DMV booklet meets both requirements. The purpose of studying the booklet is clearly to gain the knowledge necessary to pass both a written and performance test, that is, to demonstrate both the recall and application of knowledge. Whether the language tapes fill the bill will depend on what evaluation experiences they include to let the learner know if he has met a goal. (The corollary here is that the expected goal to be met must have been made clear to begin with. "Learn to speak Spanish" is not by itself testable, but "learn to select appropriate phrases for given situations" and "correctly reproduce pronunciation" of such phrases is testable within reasonable limits.) Being able to take one's blood pressure, operate the ATM or gas pump, recall the software command without referring to the information source, are performances that do indeed indicate whether learning occurred; but it was not the *expectation* of the interaction that these performances become automatic, that is, learned. Indeed, the "job aid" nature of the availability of needed information suggests that learning is not actually the expectation of either the provider or user of the information.

This distinction between learning and performance has many implications that will be explored further in later chapters.

What is the nature of self-instruction?

Situations for self-instruction

When learning is the desired outcome and expectation, how can we decide whether a self-directed learning methodology is appropriate? What situations have been shown to work well with self-instruction? What kinds of information and content have been shown to work best in a self-instructional setting?

In situations in which many individuals must learn the same information but are unable to meet as a group, self-instructional materials may provide a very practical answer to the need. An example might be a business with several branches, all expected to follow the same procedures or to possess the same knowledge of products and services. In education, the old-fashioned correspondence course has met a similar need.

Circumstances in which learners have a varied level of entry knowledge or skill but must all attain a given outcome competency are another illustration. Clearly, the time of the more-prepared students is not wasted on unnecessary re-visiting of already known material, while the less-prepared students have the opportunity to attain the same desired end goal. A business will benefit by being able to put the quicker trainee to work as soon as she is ready, and will benefit from the confidence and completeness of the learning of the trainee who needs more time. In schools, the rapid learner has the opportunity to explore a topic in greater depth, or to address other topics, and the slower learner is not rushed into missing essential knowledge or skill acquisition. (Obviously, reasonable time limits are implied in either business or school settings.) In this case, the varying time needed is the critical concern, just as in the first case, the factor of location was critical.

There are disadvantages associated with these advantages, of course: many learners feel a need for companions in the learning experience, and many learners are uneasy without an instructor to turn to. It is not easy to develop good self-instructional materials, in any delivery medium, and assessment and evaluation of self-directed learning poses some particular problems. But I have seen my students address and overcome these problems to develop sound, useful self-instructional materials. These have ranged from programmed booklets designed by a nurse-educator on particular health care problems for senior citizens, through computer-based instruction on trouble-shooting technical equipment, through factoring algebraic equations, reading maps, fire safety, exploring Greek mythology, and even incubating ostrich eggs, all representing a range of formats.

Principles of self-instruction

Regardless of topic or format, all materials designed for self-instruction require certain essential characteristics if they are to provide learners a path to the outcome they desire and assure them that they have been successful in attaining it. By far the most critical of these characteristics are the following:

Active responding. Learners must respond actively to the material being presented. Questions, choices, and interactions must be available constantly for the learner to respond to. Just reading or observing is not enough to make the presentation of information function as instruction.

PRINCIPLES OF SELF-INSTRUCTION
Active responding
Immediate feedback
Small steps
Self-pacing

Immediate feedback. Equally critical is the principle that every response is immediately followed by a consequence: the answer to a question is affirmed or corrected, a choice leads immediately to a result. These interactions go beyond the "stimulus-response" pattern of behaviorism when they represent the cognitive activity of the learners as they interact with the information.

These two core theoretical principles give rise to two core principles for the practical design of self-instructional materials: information must be presented in small enough increments to assure frequent response, and the pace at which the learner moves must be his own. *Small steps* and *self-pacing* must be included as basic characteristics of self-instruction.

These "principles of self-instruction" underlie the design and development of the self-directed learning materials and experiences which we will explore in these pages. In con-

DOMAINS OF LEARNING	
DOMAIN	TYPE OF CONTENT
Cognitive	Knowledge, thinking, acquiring, storing and using information
Affective	Feelings, preferences, values
Psychomotor	Physical and perceptual activities and skills

sidering whether self-directed learning is the methodology appropriate to a given situation, it must be possible to apply these principles effectively for this to be the approach to be selected.

Content for self instruction: Domains of learning

Probably the best known model for classifying different types of learning is that popularized by Benjamin Bloom and his collaborators in the 1950's. Bloom's taxonomy names three broad "domains" of educational outcomes: Cognitive, Affective and Psychomotor. (Some recent theorists include a fourth domain of "Interpersonal Skills.") Each of these domains may be further subdivided into categories of outcome: Bloom's initial work emphasized the Cognitive Domain, and with his colleague Kratwohl he explored the several levels of Affective outcomes in learning. (Bloom and his colleagues did not address the Psychomotor domain, and none of the taxonomies proposed by various other writers has acquired general acceptance.)

BLOOM'S TAXONOMY OF COGNITIVE OBJECTIVES	
CATEGORY	DESCRIPTION
Knowledge	Ability to recall previously learned material
Comprehension	Ability to grasp meaning, explain, restate ideas
Application	Ability to use learned material in new situations
Analysis	Ability to separate material into component parts and show relationship between parts
Synthesis	Ability to put together separate ideas to form new whole, establish new relationships
Evaluation	Ability to judge the worth of material against stated criteria

Most self-instruction occurs in the cognitive domain, or with some elements of psychomotor or task learning. Probably all learning situations have a component of the affective domain: in fact, attitude toward learning or motivation is of sufficient importance that we will consider it at some length later on.

Within the cognitive domain, it has been traditional to represent the subdivisions suggested by Bloom as a hierarchy: knowledge, comprehension, and application precede the "higher order" levels of analysis, synthesis and evaluation. Schools have been faulted for failing to pay sufficient attention to "higher order thinking skills," but this viewpoint runs the risk of undervaluing the essential basic or foundation learning which interacts with "higher order" learning. However, it is equally a mistake to place so much emphasis on "knowing the basics" that using, analyzing or evaluating these "basics" is overlooked or not included in instruction.

The hierarchical model may not really be appropriate as a way to represent the connections between the different kinds of learning. Perhaps concentric circles would be a better picture of the way different kinds of thinking about a topic or task relate to each other. Even better would be a model recognizing the "ripple" effect of deepening understanding, like a stone cast into water, sending out ripples which expand and intersect and unite the different kinds and levels of cognitive activity set up by the initiating idea.

It may be helpful to consider some examples of cognitive activity of the different kinds Bloom identifies. What are learners doing when the are thinking at the knowledge level, or the analysis level? Many texts have presented lists of verbs associated with Bloom's categories. A sample is shown in the box on the following page.

In the practical work of developing instructional activities for a classroom, such lists can be very useful guides for developing tasks and materials. Providing some student activity for each level can help greatly to assure a more indepth consideration of whatever topic is being taught. Of course, it is not the choice of verb to describe an activity which determines the

VERBS FOR LEVELS OF THE COGNITIVE DOMAIN			
Knowledge	arrange list	name label	repeat match
Comprehension	explain translate	review express	describe locate
Application	demonstrate solve	use illustrate	operate schedule
Analysis	categorize distinguish	diagram select	compare contrast
Synthesis	compose formulate	construct design	plan assemble
Evaluation	rate support	appraise judge	predict score

cognitive level at which the student will work:
the carefully thought-out nature of the mental
process involved is what determines the actual
level of functioning. However, as a how-to
guide for practical lesson development,
Bloom's taxonomy and a familiar verb list can
be a very real help, in designing self-directed
learning as well as class instruction.

Kinds of content

The information content upon which people
may exercise these mental processes has also
been classified by various researchers into categories which are helpful to the planning of instruction. Merrill (1983) has developed a taxonomy of information types named as "Facts,

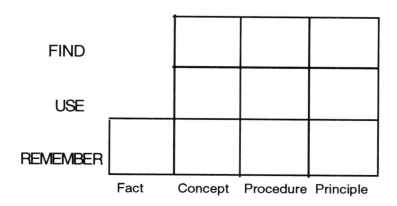

FIND

USE

REMEMBER

Fact   Concept   Procedure   Principle

Merrill: Types Of Content, Levels Of Performance

Concepts, Procedures, Principles." The broad processes for interacting with these kinds of information he terms "Remember, Use, Find," terminology which roughly parallels and condenses Bloom.

Similarly, Robert Gagne (1985) has suggested that learning outcomes may be grouped into the broad categories of verbal information, intellectual skills, cognitive strategies, motor skills and attitudes. The first three outcome categories roughly parallel Bloom's "Cognitive Domain." The subdivisions that Gagne names for "intellectual skills" identify the various kinds of information content for instruction as discriminations, concrete concepts, defined concepts, rules, and higher order rules. Again, we can see parallels with both Bloom and Merrill in the concept of increasing complexity

LEARNING OUTCOMES (GAGNE)	
Verbal Information	Names or labels, statement of fact, organized information
Intellectual Skills	Discriminations, concrete concepts, defined concepts, rules, higher-order rules
Cognitive Strategies	Attention strategies, encoding strategies, retrieval strategies
Motor Skills	Procedures, performance of tasks involving use of senses and the body
Attitude	Internal beliefs, feelings and preferences, associated behaviors

of cognitive function for differing types of content, and a further reminder that attitudinal outcomes are an inseparable component of our presentation of information on any topic which may be affected by the way we design the learning experience.

Finally, a distinction can be made as to whether the content for planned instruction is topic or task, knowledge or skill which is to be developed. It is useful to ask yourself what kind of question the instructional experience is intended to answer: are the learners asking What? How? or Why? about the information to be considered. A combination of the approaches discussed above may help you reach the content decisions you must make for designing any kind of instruction, and for determining effective presentation for self-instruction.

Expository/inquiry delivery styles

In making the determination of delivery format, we address a major question: is the delivery style we select for our self-instructional learning to be *expository or inquiry-based?* M. David Merrill's writings on Component Display Theory (1983) and subsequent Component Design Theory explore the difference in emphasis of these two orientations. These differing approaches afford two perspectives from which to address the question posed earlier: "What is there that instruction does to information that makes it different, that facilitates learning?"

Basically, expository instruction is tutorial in format. The instructional material presents information to the student, assures opportunity for the student's interaction and practice, and determines through careful questioning whether the student's replies and actions indicate understanding. Errors will be corrected and the student led as fully as possible to mastery of the material. In tutorial self-instruction, as with a human tutor, the learner actively answers questions about the information presented and responds to directions to reach the intended outcome. Essentially, the emphasis is placed on what the "tutor" does to direct the learner to the desired ends, to help the learner find good answers.

In contrast, the inquiry-based format places its emphasis on what the *learner* does to move toward the desired outcome. Instructional simulations, in which the learner must investigate a body of information to arrive at answers, illustrate this approach. The instruction must assure that all necessary information is available, and the instruction must answer the learner's questions. "What happens if I do this?" must lead to a clear result from which the learner draws the conclusions and makes the connections that constitute the learning outcome. The inquiry style is sometimes called "experiential" when the instruction provides experiences for the learner, and this style may also be referred to as "exploratory." The emphasis is upon the designer helping the learner frame good questions to direct his way through the learning experience.

There are theoretical and practical considerations underlying both delivery styles which we will investigate further. These viewpoints are sometimes argued in the literature as opposing philosophies, but I do not believe they are necessarily antithetical. The decision about delivery style need not be "either-or" but may well appropriately combine the elements of each which will best match the other instructional design considerations which must go into planning and designing self-directed learning.

Summary

Designing self-instruction is a special case of the broad profession of Instructional Design. It poses special challenges and offers special opportunities to the designer who seeks to provide a learning experience which is largely directed by the learners themselves. To do so, the designer must assure that the intended outcome of the instruction is what the learner assumes it to be. (In some circumstances, the designer may also need to convince the learner of the usefulness and interest of the instructional experience.) The instructional materials and activities for self-instruction require a high degree of interaction and must provide learners with constant feedback as they monitor their progress.

Whatever the content, good instruction encourages learners to work beyond simple recall or recognition of information to a level of understanding which will enable them to apply and build on their new knowledge or skills. Finally, self-instruction provides learners the opportunity to assess their attained learning against the outcome they anticipated. The challenge of developing instruction which will foster the active partnership of the learners and successfully guide them to the desired goal is a demanding but stimulating enterprise for the instructional designer.

REFERENCES AND SUGGESTIONS FOR FURTHER RELATED READING

Alessi, S. M., & Trollip, S. R. (1991). Computer-based instruction: Methods and development. (2nd ed.). Englewood Cliffs, NJ: Prentice Hall.

Bloom, B. S., Engelhart, M. D., Hill, W. H., Furst, E. J. & Kratwohl, Dr. R. (1956). Taxonomy of educational objectives, Handbook I: Cognitive domain. New York: McKay. Reprinted (1972) by Longman, New York.

Gagne, R. (1985). Conditions of learning. (4th edition). New York: Holt, Rinehart & Winston.

Kemp, J. E. (1985). The instructional design process. New York: Harper & Row.

Kemp, J. E.; Morrison, G. R., & Ross, S. M. (1996). Designing effective instruction,. (2nd Ed.) Upper Saddle River, NJ: Merrill-Prentice Hall.

Kratwohl, D. R., Bloom, B. S., & Masia, B. B. (1964). Taxonomy of educational objectives. Handbook II: Affective Domain. New York: McKay.

Markle, S. M. (1981). Designs for instructional designers. Champaign, IL: Stipes.

Merrill, M. D. (1983). Component display theory. In Reigeluth, C. M. (Ed.) Instructional design theories and models. Hillsdale, NJ: Erlbaum.

Merrill, M. D. (1990). In Twitchell, D. (Ed.) Robert M. Gagne and M. David Merrill: In conversation. Educational Technology, Vol. #, p. 37.

Romiszowski, A. J. (1986). <u>Developing auto-instructional materials.</u> New York: Nichols.

Rossett, A. (1987). <u>Training needs assessment.</u> Englewood Cliffs, NJ: Educational Technology Publications.

Chapter Two: Expository Self-Instruction —The Good Tutorial

In working with information for learning outcomes, a primary consideration must be that not all learners or learning settings are appropriate for self-instruction. The careful analysis of learners, settings, and content which precedes all professional instructional design activities is particularly important for self-instruction because often the instructional material provides either all or nearly all of the learner's interaction with the content to be learned. The nature of the learning situation will contribute to the decision to employ either an expository or inquiry focus.

In considering delivery format, we are all aware that technology is increasingly extending the range of possibilities for presenting and responding to information in learning situations, but high-end systems are far from universally available, either in schools or business and industry. The available delivery system may itself limit the range of possible interactions to be offered to the learner. Good instruction must work with what is possible. In any medium, the presentation of the information must reflect our professional awareness of the characteristics and attributes of the medium itself as well as the characteristics and attributes of the learners and the content to be learned.

Of the two delivery styles considered earlier, the more familiar is the expository, or tutorial, "explain-and-check-for-understanding" style. Many learning and training situations expect the transfer of a body of established knowledge and/or set of skills from "expert" to novice. Very commonly in training situations, this transfer takes the form of someone who knows how to do a task showing the trainee what the process is, and then having the trainee replicate the steps while being checked by the expert for correctness.

In academic settings, this delivery style assumes the form of a teacher presenting information, and then asking questions of the learners which are designed to assess the retention and comprehension of the information by those learners. When well done, an expository delivery style employs a range of appropriate presentation media, and questioning covers the range of Bloom's taxonomy in the responses expected. The expository format follows the pattern identified by Alessi and Trollip (1991) as encompassing the following four stages:

> Presenting information
> Guiding the student
> Practicing by the student
> Assessing student learning

As these comments suggest, expository instruction may be group-based, or an individual may work with a single tutor. In recent years, both vocational and academic training in this style for the individual learner have been produced in various formats, including print and assorted media packages. The most current application of individualized tutorial packages is seen in computer-based materials.

Historical background of Expository Self-Instruction

We can trace the rise of the self-instructional tutorial to roots in the work of various earlier educational psychologists. E. L. Thorndike, of Columbia University Teachers College, theorized in the early 1900's that certain conditions govern learning and may be manipulated to maximize learning. The most important of Thorndike's laws is the law of effect, which states that the connection of a response to a given stimulus will be strengthened only if the some success or satisfaction follows the response. The connection would be decreased, in Thorndike's view, if the result of the response is unpleasant. Thorndike further noted that stimulus-response associations are strengthened through repetition, (the law of exercise), and that the most recent response is the most likely to govern the recurrence (the law of recency.)

In the 1920's, Sydney Pressey at Ohio State University developed a "teaching machine" which he considered applied the laws of effect and also of recency. His device consisted of box with a window for information and four keys that the user pressed to select the answer to a question presented, with four possible answers, in the window.

This machine was actually a testing machine, as the information presented would have been studied previously by the learner who used the machine. If the student selected the correct answer, the machine turned the cylinder within and presented a new question. If the answer was incorrect, nothing happened and the student was forced to select again. Thus, providing the correct answer had the satisfactory effect of acknowledging the student's understanding and moving him forward. Since the last answer selected in any sequence had to be the correct one, the law of recency applied. In one version of his machine, Pressey arranged that the student would be required to answer each question correctly twice during the sequence of questions, thus applying the law of exercise. However, Pressey's high hopes for his machine went unfulfilled as the depression and then war years followed his invention of the device.

Programmed Instruction

Linear programs

It was in the 1950's that the behavioral psychologist B. F. Skinner turned his research from laboratory experiments in shaping and conditioning animal behavior to an interest in the implications of his work for humans. His investigation of the stimulus-response connections in animal subjects led him to look into the stimulus-response connection in human behavior, especially the complex chains of behavior seen in learning situations.

Skinner developed a form of expository presentation that is known as "linear programming." In this technique, a student is presented with a small amount of information which provides the stimulus, and is immediately asked to respond to the stimulus by construction of a response. Care is taken, and in a few good examples of early linear programs, great ingenuity is used, to assure that the learner must pay real attention to the stimulus and that his response will be the correct one. A principal point to note is that the linear program does not allow the learner to select from possible answers, in order to avoid the possibility of any connection being made between the stimulus and a wrong response. This principle of "errorless learning" is a core tenet of the linear form of program.

To assure that a program led learners to form the correct responses, it became an accepted and expected part of program development to test programmed material on sample audiences in order to identify steps which allowed error on the part of the learner. It became a principle that "if the learner makes a mistake, it is not his fault but the fault of the program." This requirement for rigorous student testing of materials, while perhaps not always strictly followed, is a major contribution of the programmed instruction movement to current instructional design practice. Today focus is no longer on developing errorless materials, but the testing of materials by example students from the prospective audience is one of the strong points of truly systematic ID, one which may be considered a fifth "principle" for designing self-instruction.

Skinner's ideas caught the attention not only of educators in schools but of people charged with training in business and the military. Grants for research into programming techniques fostered considerable work during the 1950's. Numerous teaching machines and pro-

PRINCIPLES OF SELF-INSTRUCTION
Active Responding Immediate Feedback Small Steps Self-Pacing
Testing by Students

grams were developed to apply Skinner's instructional techniques. Instructional books were published which presented the information stimulus on one side of a page, while the learner covered the responses on the other side with a "slider" of some kind, forming his response before pulling down the slider to receive the reinforcement of seeing the correct response.

Programmed instruction developed a large following. Good Frames and Bad (1964), by Susan Meyer Markle, a pupil of Skinner, is the classic description of the techniques of linear programming.

Branching programs

By the end of the 1950's, some researchers began to question the "errorless" emphasis of linear programming. Norman Crowder, an instructor for the Air Force, is credited with the introduction in about 1958 of the so-called "branching" program, a form of programmed material that asked for responses to its frames in the form of multiple choice questions. A correct selection of the answer sent learners on to the next frame of information, but the selection of a wrong answer directed them to a different page upon which the error was explained and the information re-presented, with another chance to select the correct answer.

This fundamentally different conception of the effect of error as a diagnostic tool to improve learning led to the development of programs of instruction in the "scrambled book" format as well as to materials for various brands of so-called teaching machines.

Computer programs

However, the basic awkwardness of print as a medium for either format, and the limited usefulness of specific machines, eventually led to the fading of interest in the use of programmed instructional materials in most areas of education and training. As a delivery style, programs of instruction lay dormant until the appearance of the computer, and even more, the microcomputer, brought these techniques to the attention of developers once more.

The very nature of the computer, with its fixed-size screen and the need for input from the user for its functioning matched the emphasis of programmed instruction upon small steps, active responding, and immediate feedback. The ability of the computer to accept user input as answers to questions and to compare these responses to possible answers within the program seemed to promise a marriage between the constructed response of linear programming and the diagnostic usefulness of branching programming. In recent years, there has been a huge surge of development in computer-assisted instruction, often taking advantage of the record-keeping capacity of the machine and of the computer's branching capability in meeting individual learner's needs.

It should be noted here that both linear and branching styles of presenting programmed material to the learner are basically expository. The assumption is made that the learner reads

or otherwise observes the information provided, and the program then asks a question to
determine how well the information has been
understood. This is the traditional, tutorial approach to instruction which functions to transfer knowledge and skill from the expert to the
novice, and to assess the level of comprehension as the result of the instruction.

In contrast to this technique is the style of instruction sometimes called "discovery learning" which we have seen encourages the
learner to explore a body of information, ask
questions and form conclusions. However,
Skinner himself noted (1986) that setting up
learning activities which direct learners to dis-
cover a pre-planned outcome is hardly more
than a variation on the method of direct explanation.

The implications of inquiry-based learning situations will be explored more fully in the later
sections of this book: there is no suggestion
that either style for developing instruction is
superior. Indeed, the decision to select one type
or the other must be part of the rigorous analysis that precedes all good instructional design,
and the basic planning considerations are vir-
tually identical for the design of learning experiences in both formats.

Recall too that we noted earlier a number of
reasons for people to interact with a body of information: sometimes people need information only at a particular point in time, to make
a choice or decision, or to accomplish a tempo-

rary task. Designing a good information kiosk or a good "job aid" is a useful and valid professional task, but it is different from designing good self-instruction. This book addresses the situation in which *learning* is the intended result of the development of interactions with information, the situation indicating the need for good self-instruction designed in either of these two styles.

Let us consider first, then, what are the strengths of good expository instruction and in what circumstances it is particularly appropriate as a design methodology for self-instruction.

Designing Expository instruction: Fundamental Considerations

Considerations for content and learners

A very wide range of content is appropriate for expository self-instruction. One may develop tutorials to provide instruction in factual information, procedures, rules, principles or problem-solving strategies (Alessi & Trollip, 1991). Perhaps the one kind of learning outcome unlikely to work well in this form is Bloom's "synthesis" level. Because true synthesis involves creating something new from elements that have been taught, feedback is very difficult and often impossible without active human interaction.

Yet we need to remember that from the learner's point of view, when he does not know the outcome, his mental functioning is in fact at the analysis, synthesis or evaluation level as he investigates the information provided and seeks appropriate results. Furthermore, well-designed practice activities in an expository lesson can provide application level outcomes that afford the learner experiences quite close to synthesis. Such synthesis may occur in work or school situations after the lesson is concluded and its objectives are transferred to the practical world. At present, all the delivery systems available to us are too limited to respond to novelty as a live instructor can.

Considerations for process

The ideal instructional situation is sometimes described as one student and a good tutor. Bloom (1984) refers to "the best learning conditions that we can devise, *tutoring...*" (Emphasis ours.) Designing self-instruction puts the designer in the position of functioning as the tutor: what do we need to do to assure being a good tutor?

We noted earlier that the basic structure of an expository lesson has the following elements:

Presenting information
Guiding the student
Practicing by the student
Assessing student learning

Good classroom instruction addresses each of these elements effectively. For example, considerations for presenting information include decisions about vocabulary and phrasing, about whether graphics or sound will aid in communicating the intended message, and for spoken presentation, all the issues of tone, intonation, gesture and so on with which teachers and trainers are used to dealing. Clarity and focus are important components of effective presentation of information.

The guiding of learners often takes place in a good classroom lesson through questioning and feedback as learners are included in and involved in the presentation of information by the teacher. Correction of misunderstandings and affirmation of appropriate responses keep learners on the right track as they take in the new information.

A good classroom expository lesson includes within it, or as follow-up, or both, the opportunity to practice with the newly learned concepts or skills. And finally, an opportunity is given to the learner to show that he has in fact succeeded in learning the lesson material through a testing situation.

Although testing in schools may identify unsuccessful learners as well, no worthwhile lesson is ever taught with the *intention* that some of the students will fail. Good expository teaching aims at helping the learner learn, and teachers who are good at this style of teaching usually exhibit the behaviors identified by

Rosenshine (1983) as recommended to improve student achievement:

Proceed in small steps . . . but at a rapid pace.

Use high frequency of questions and overt student practice.

Give feedback to students, particularly when they are correct but hesitant.

Make corrections by simplifying questions, giving clues, explaining or reviewing steps or reteaching lost steps.

The parallels between these effective classroom teaching behaviors and the principles which we have seen as guiding the development of good self-instruction are obvious. Once we are reasonably confident that the subject to be taught is feasible, and that an established need for instruction exists for our intended learners, we can move on to take the necessary steps to set up the implied contract upon which the design of self-instruction rests.

Establishing the "Implied Contract"

We begin with the basic assumption that the expected Instructional Design step of a thorough front-end analysis has been taken, with consideration of the learning situation, prospective learners, and content to be taught. We will next look at the steps in the process of planning and designing a self-directed learning experience. However, it should be noted that designing for self-instruction, like other areas of Instructional Design, is an iterative process, revisiting and elaborating as appropriate on the steps taken earlier as the process unfolds.

Analysis provides us with a picture both of where the learners are now and what the picture would look like if the desired learning takes place. We have said that instruction differs from simply informing in that people bring to an instructional situation an intent to learn what is to be presented to them. It is therefore necessary that prospective learners have a clear description of what is to be learned at the very outset of the instruction.

The outcomes of the learning experience may be stated as goals or more specifically as objectives: some educators prefer broader, more open statements, while others emphasize clear definition of the cognitive or observable performances the learner will acquire. Let us look at what is involved in informing learners of this essential component of the "implied contract," that is, letting them know where the instruction will take them if they sign on for it.

Objectives

Objectives have traditionally been statements of what the learner will be able to <u>do</u> after instruction. A frequently used mnemonic for the components of an objective is the "ABCD" list of Audience, Behavior, Conditions, and Degree (Knirk & Gustafson, 1986). These elements make a useful guide for direct instruction in many settings, but they have

ABCD's OF OBJECTIVES
Audience
Behavior
Conditions
Degree

some limitations which we need to consider, especially for self-instructional situations.

Audience

Clearly, different characteristics of the learner audience will require different teaching decisions with regard to the nature and presentation of content, the choice of activities and expected levels of knowledge or skill resulting from the lesson or course. Thoughtful consideration of *who* will be the learners for the planned instruction is vital to any form of instructional planning.

Behavior: overt/covert

Let us note also that the term "Behavior" must be considered in its broadest sense. Mager (1984) points out in his book on objectives that the designer must recognize and state the real intent of the learning outcome: the "behaviors" aimed for should represent the new mental performance capabilities which the learner will acquire. Our understanding of human learning has moved from a focus on purely observable performances to a view more oriented to cognitive considerations. Thus, the hidden or "covert" mental action is what the learner really needs to be able to do. However, this covert performance can be illustrated by various "overt" or "indicator" behaviors.

For example, try doing the following things, without putting down this book or saying anything aloud:
add 37 and 22;
spell Mississippi;
identify learning resources in this room;
compose a couplet about yourself.

All these are covert: did you do them? How would an observer tell that you had? Try to think of more than one indicator behavior for each. (For instance, you could say the answer to the addition problem or write it in a workbook; list or point out or name the learning resources, etc.) Clearly, it is not the indicator action which you "learned to do," but the covert cognitive action which is the true learning outcome.

SOME COGNITIVE PERFORMANCE VERBS WHICH UNDERLIE INDICATOR ACTIONS		
Identify	Classify	Distinguish
Recognize	Check	Compare
Plan	Locate	Sequence
Interpret	Predict	Relate
Select	Offer	Compute
Compose	Determine	Analyze

For our purposes, note that this suggestion means stating objectives meaningful enough to be demonstrated in more than one narrow way. A meaningful skill or useful knowledge can be applied in various contexts.

Increasingly, both education and training settings are looking at a systems approach to managing learning. Learning is being recognized as an ongoing process, with specific objectives or outcomes as milestones along the way. In 1990, W. Edwards Deming, the well-known expert on quality commented, "Job-training alone is not enough...everyone has to understand where they're going." Thus, as we plan for self-instruction, we should concentrate on the framing of the statements of the covert, mental, cognitive outcomes of instruction which help our learners understand what they can expect as milestones along the way through the learning experience they are about to enter.

Near or far transfer

However, we should remember that certain training situations may suggest that broad, cognitive objectives are too vague. Operating a particular kind of equipment, for example, may well require very focused statements of outcomes in order to guide the learner to the proper performance of specific duties he needs to be able to do right now. Piskurich (1993) advises that the designer do a very careful analysis of the job or task to be taught, and to name as objectives for the learner the ability to

INDICATOR BEHAVIOR OBJECTIVE	REAL INTENT VERB(S)
For each of the following symptoms, be able to name the appropriate analgesic.	
Write your estimate of the time involved for each step in the process, in order.	
Sort the fabric samples into three stacks representing fiber content.	
Label the blank map with the names of the states shown.	
Number the stations on the route to represent the shortest feasible driving time.	
Back the vehicle through a 1/4 mile coned course on the parking lot within 5 minutes without knocking over any of the cones.	

ACTIVITY

What "real intent""could underlie these "indicator behaviors?" Select from the cognitive verb list presented earlier. More than one may be appropriate: you be the judge.

perform each step in the procedure as necessary with the particular materials and in the particular setting the trainee will work in. Very direct instruction promotes the "near" transfer of learning, which may be the goal your analysis determines is appropriate for the self-instruction you are to design.

However, if you think of the performance for the particular task as representing the trainee's understanding of her job rather than rote memorization of the activities it involves, you will find it useful to identify the covert ability which underlies the overt actions of the successful learner and state both in the objectives.

Finally, a real consideration in the present day world is the rapid change in job activities. A learner working with a word processor document who can "use the 'find' command to locate all references to a given supplier" will be more likely to transfer that ability to a new version of the word processor than the learner who is taught "press F5" to locate all such references, if the new version has a different indicator action for the "find" process. (And only part of the self-instructional materials will need to be changed for the new training, too.)

<u>Conditions and Degree</u>

A final consideration for self-instruction is that the nature of the conditions under which the learner is working may vary and cannot always be specified in the instructional material. Similarly, imposing degrees such as "within fifteen minutes" or "with no more than two re-tries" is not useful when there is no way for these aspects to be directly assessed. (Such skill levels could be suggested to the learner as the guidelines for assessing his own developing ability, however.)

The planning pyramid

A very powerful technique to help decide upon the objectives for a block of instruction is the use of a top-down approach to analyzing the intended learning. Peter Pipe (1966) uses the term "Pyramid of Objectives" for this planning style. I use the term with full credit to his core idea, which was extremely influential to my own learning and which I have for years taught to my students. Decide how you will state the overall outcome of your planned instruction in a clear but comprehensive form. Then ask yourself, "What would a learner have to be able to do before he could do *that?*" Try to identify the next most critical and comprehensive ability or abilities that underlie the final skill. Then look critically at the next-to-the-top objective or objectives, and again ask yourself, "What would they have to be able to do in order to do *that*?"

IMPORTANT TO NOTE

Note carefully here that this process is not analyzing the steps in a task but analyzing the cognitive process underlying the performance of the task. You are trying to build a "pyramid of objectives," not the *steps in a procedure.*

Let's look at a simple example. Our end competency is that the learner will be able to "Produce a document using a desktop publishing software program."

What is the skill or cluster of skills that would immediately precede "production?" The final thing you have to know how to do in this case is to "be able to print the document."

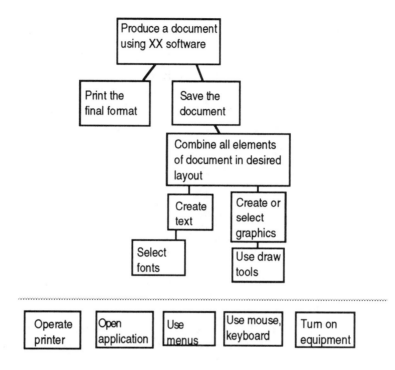

As you go on down the example levels, you find skills which are both essential to the step above, but which could be learned in any order. Such objectives are on a coordinate level, and when you decide on the teaching/learning activities to go with each objective, you can decide which you want to begin with, or offer the learner the choice of which he wants to begin with. When you get to the "be able to" level such as "load software" or "use menus" which is prerequisite to the content you want to teach, you are through with your pyramid. You are now ready to start at the bottom of the diagram and develop the sequential content

outline which will lead your learners to the
end outcome.

The planning pyramid has the added benefit of
helping you identify learning activities or steps
in the task being learned which often may present themselves as objectives in the first planning stage. For example, for the overall objective of "Producing a document with such and
such a software program," one step in the task
is "Put paper in the printer tray." Since it is
part of the task, isn't it an objective? Not
unless the loading of the paper tray has
enough possible variations that knowing how
to "put the *appropriate* paper in the tray
correctly"is actually something the learner will
have to "be able" to do. As you lay out your
plan, determining objectives and how to assess
them, you will have to decide which steps in
attaining the desired knowledge or skill are
actually meaningful outcomes, sufficiently
significant to deserve statement as objectives,
and which steps are subsumed in those
objectives. Keep your pyramid lean,
comprehensive, and focused on objectives
rather than activities to help you establish a
solid planning structure.

Fulfilling the "implied contract"

Assessing attainment; evaluation

At the other end of the implied contract is the
opportunity for learners to determine whether

and how well they have met the objectives they purposefully undertook to strive for. In the self-instructional situation, learners must be able to evaluate their own progress, as there is ordinarily no teacher to do so and no peers to compare to. Thus, issues in assessment and evaluation are the second important design consideration for the implied contract.

Many authors suggest deciding on how an objective will be measured at the time the objective itself is determined. This can be a useful practice as it provides both a start and a finish line for planning the instructional activities that will take the learner through the content to the desired new knowledge and skills. Ideas for content presentation and often decisions about the necessary level of detail for the instruction can arise from this process.

It will also help you locate "objectives" which are so narrow as to be either learning activities or themselves test questions. If you find yourself trying to think of a test question for an objective which states "the learner will be able to list the five steps in the inspection process," I submit you need to ask yourself what meaningful learning is represented by being able to write such a list. The list may be an indicator of the ability to organize process steps in proper sequence, and such a question might indeed provide the learner a check on whether or not he can correctly sequence the steps. But listing is not the objective; sequencing is. As such, there will more than one way to check it out. Maybe writing the list will be the assessment question you decide on, but do not confuse the indicator with the real intent.

Criterion questions

With the objective stated, you need to decide what question, correctly answered, would show mastery of that objective. Such a summary question is termed the "criterion" question. Paper or on-line questions to be answered, checklists to mark, or such testing activities as putting an X on the parts of a picture (clicking on elements, if you are computer-based) can let the learner know whether she meets criterion.

Sometimes the familiar forms of test questions do not seem adequate to assess mastery of an objective. You may need a criterion *activity*. Perhaps the learner could be asked to sketch components in correct relationships or drag them with a mouse on a computer. Another approach might be presenting a scenario and asking the learner to identify elements of a learned skill, or to re-arrange steps or substitute better choices of actions for those given in the scenario.

Clearly the principle of immediate feedback becomes a concern here. A sample sketch with critical points emphasized must let the learner check if he too has included all critical points. (Computer feedback can be more precise.) Is the learner required to identify all of the elements in the scenario or enough to indicate acceptable mastery? What level is to be considered acceptable? The feedback will have to identify all possible elements and allow the learner to compare his selection to that list and figure whether he has matched the necessary number.

When a range— albeit a narrow range— of possible answers would meet the criterion, you must work very carefully to determine what appropriate and informative feedback will tell learners that their response shows the necessary level of understanding. In the headline scenario below, for instance, you may need to tell learners which three actions *had* to be changed and suggest synonyms for the choices of actions which would indicate improvement so that learners can check their choices against the acceptable range.

Finally, in some circumstances (for example, a training program for bank clerks), the unit of self-instruction leads up to a performance which must be formally evaluated by someone else. However, the information and practice which the tutorial provides should assure the learner that he can confidently *expect* to perform at a criterion level as a result of working through the instruction, that he possesses the readiness to show that he can perform as desired. Self-instruction can well be a *part of* a learning situation: it does not always have to be the whole thing. We will reconsider issues in performance assessment when we look at part two, simulations and experiential type instruction.

A SCENARIO: MODIFYING HEADLINES

EVALUATION FRAME FOR THE SCENARIO

Now that you have learned about writing good headlines and had some practice writing a headline, let's check how well you are doing. Make a better headline out of the following:

"Administrator announces that make-up examinations will no longer be offered after finals week."

Underline three words or phrases that need changing and then write your improved headline below.

Your new headline:

FEEDBACK FOR THE EVALUATION FRAME

The words you should have underlined as needing change in that example of writing a headline would be "announces," "examinations" and "will no longer be offered".

If your new headline says something like, "Principal says no more late exams" or "Principal halts late tests," you have the right idea.

Example Evaluation and Feedback Frame

As you can see, writing meaningful objectives which lead to meaningful evaluations is no small challenge. A good tutorial addresses this challenge at the outset, in the initial design phase, as all aspects of establishing the "implied contract" are considered.

Developing Expository Self Instruction: Presenting Information

Content Analysis

With objectives and assessment providing the starting and ending points for the tutorial, we can now consider more directly what instructional material and activities to present to our learners. Let's reconsider what kind of content this instruction covers: where do the objectives lead to new knowledge, where to new skill primarily? Are you dealing with a topic that your learners must know about, or a task they must learn to do? Where in the information you need to present will learners be asking "What?" or "Why?" Where in the information will they be seeking to find out "How?" Presenting information and activities that will help them answer those questions is the next major focus of developing a good tutorial.

Thus, if you find you are teaching a task, you will need to analyze it carefully to see what the steps in successful completion of the task will be. At the same time, you will need to consider carefully what the learner needs to know *about* in order to do each step. For instance, learning how to take properly exposed photographs requires knowing the steps in the process and also knowing about the concepts of shutter speed, lens opening, and the relationships expressed in the rules about depth of field.

Similarly, if you find you are teaching mainly concepts or principles, you will need to consider the various tasks people need to do in coming to understand the content. The concept learning of the names of all the bones in the body includes learning the tasks of categorizing and discriminating and arranging the information into meaningful groups. When you develop a list of steps for a task, and a parallel list of "know about" content knowledge for the steps, you can begin to group up the actual blocks of information you need to present to the learner who is undertaking to learn this task and this content.

Assuring Active Responding: Today's "small steps"

We have established that information in self-instructional material is presented in "small steps." What kind of block of information constitutes a "small step?" The term used by writers of programmed instruction was "frames." Susan Markle's classic "Good Frames and Bad" (1964) addressed major considerations for presenting text (and appropriate graphics, but mainly text) in the short, coherent blocks to be called "frames" in paper-based material.

When programmed materials moved to computers, the "screen" of information became the term, and issues of fitting information into the confines of a particular screen size became paramount. As computers rapidly became more sophisticated and color and graphics became available, "screen design" concerns received developers' attention.

Today's technology affords designers and learners such multimedia possibilities as sound and motion, which add the issue of duration of time to the concept of small step. "How long" is a small step, as well as "how big" becomes a concern. Now we have "stacks" of "cards" which represent the current terminology for small steps, and increasingly web-based materials are presented in "pages" which can link to other "pages."

Whatever we call them, organization of information into coherent and meaningful units is a challenge to the designer of such material. The traditional term "frame" is used from here on to refer this concept. Whether in simple or elaborate format, the really major point about writing self-instructional material is that every "frame" must be structured so as to elicit a meaningful response.

A frame of information is not like a good paragraph in a composition or report. We learned that such a paragraph has a clear topic sentence, followed by the development of ideas leading to a summary sentence. Such a paragraph tells information effectively but does not require a response. Good students often highlight the key ideas as they read text, to be sure, thereby responding to the information, but a frame of information faces the challenge of getting the learner to come up with the key idea, to construct or identify rather than mark or copy the significant concepts presented. Highlighting is insufficiently involving to count as active responding: real mental processing of the information is the goal of a good frame.

Some examples may clarify this point. A course in database fundamentals introduces such basic terms as file, record and field. A sample section might be:

Data is not information until it is organized in some meaningful and coherent fashion. Database systems group data into categories at three levels: the file, the record and the field. A file is a collection of records, like your personal address book which consists of several items of information about each person in the book. The page of information about each person is a record, the specific items of information are the fields in the record.

An address book is a_____

_____

Each page is a _____

_____

Each piece of information for a person is a_____

The requested response is a possibility. It is quite straightforward: learners might learn the terms by copying them down in this manner. A better and more active response would get them to apply their understanding of the frame's information: what do you think of that might work? Form your idea, and then look at the next page to see a suggestion.

Data is not information until it is organized in some meaningful and coherent fashion. Database systems group data into categories at three levels: the file, the record and the field. A file is a collection of records, like your personal address book which consists of several items of information about each person in the book. The page of information about each person is a record, the specific items of information are the fields in the record.

How would you organize a family birthday list?

The file would be _____
Each record would be _____
Some fields you would need would be _____

Better response to the data base frame

Here is another sample, presenting quite different content for a quite different audience, but illustrating the same principle of eliciting active responding.

"Latitude" and "longitude" are the names of the lines that divide the globe into sections. It is easy to remember that lines of <u>longitude</u> go the <u>long</u> way over the globe, from top to bottom. Lines of latitude go around the globe, starting with the equator which divides the globe equally into two halves at the middle.

What do we call the "Long way" lines? _____
What do we call the lines around the globe ?_____
What is the name of the line in the middle?_____

Young learners might learn the terms in this way, but this type of "copy" response is weak. What might be more actively involving here, more likely to help them connect the definition with its representation? A suggestion for an improved form follows.

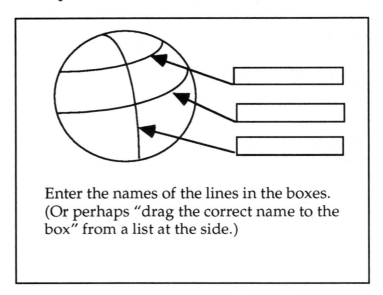

Enter the names of the lines in the boxes. (Or perhaps "drag the correct name to the box" from a list at the side.)

Better response to the geography frame

More common for new writers of frames (or cards or screens) is the kind of problem posed by the next material. As written, the paragraph tells the main point, leaving the learner nothing to do in response to it. How can you change the presentation of the information to cause the learner to process the information and by his own thinking construct the main point?

Edmund Halley first observed the comet that would later bear his name in the winter of 1682-83. After years of calculating, he decided that the comet reported in 1531 and the comet seen in 1607 were probably identical to the 1682-83 comet. From his calculations, he decided his comet had an elliptical orbit and would return every 76 years. He asked young astronomers to watch the skies in 1758-59 and see if his figures would prove correct.

First, what is the main point as you see it? The intention was that the 76 year periodicity of the comet is the idea here. A more effective frame would encourage learners to process the information presented and generate the main idea themselves. Students have revised this frame in class exercises to something similar to the following:

Edmund Halley first observed the comet that would later bear his name in the winter of 1682-83. After years of calculating, he decided that the comet seen in 1531 and the comet reported in 1607 were similar and probably identical to the 1682-83 comet, returning regularly to our view as it moved in an elliptical orbit around the sun. In what year did he predict the next return of what we now call "Halley's Comet?" _____

This kind of response requires the learner to carefully note the information and to do the calculating of the period from the available data; in short, to respond actively. We can see that the designer will also need to assure feedback to affirm or correct the response in all such active interactions. This point remains true for alternate formats of interactions such as pointing and clicking in which the designer must provide meaningful options and associated feedback as guidance for continuing.

While simply copying an idea is insufficiently active responding, neither is it our intent to engage the learners in trying to solve a puzzle. Be careful not to foster a guessing game by offering unclear choices or too-open constructions. A "Wheel of Fortune" response or an irrelevantly tricky question are not active responding either.

Two Poor Response Formats

Halley's comet has an _____ _____
around the _____ and returns every _____
_____.

Halley's comet was seen in   a. 1531, 1607, 1683
                                     b. 1513, 1670, 1638
                                     c. 1500, 1576, 1652

Considerations for format

Graphic design is a field in itself. The designer organizing information for self-instructional materials may find the following brief suggestions a help in making the form of the information help it convey its message.

The arrangement of information is a critical aspect of the degree to which it communicates the intended message. For text displays, the choice of type font contributes to readability or emphasis. Fonts are termed "serif" type fonts if the letters have small extension lines to the basic letter shape. The text of this book, Palatino, is a serif font. It was selected because serif fonts are considered to help readers readily follow the flow of text from one word to the next. In contrast, "sans-serif" fonts are those which do not have such extensions. Note that the headings for this book and text within some boxes are set in sans-serif fonts, which tend to focus emphasis upon a short message or even individual words more effectively. Very elaborate fonts can get in the way of conveying information by calling attention to themselves rather than to the text they present.

Similarly, an emphasis on terms to be recalled in later responses can be shown by selecting an emphatic type face in which to introduce them. Boldface, italics or underlining used when the term is presented call attention to it and make it stand out from the background text. This is a small but useful kind of "prompt" to readers' attention.

Arranging a series of words or phrases in a vertical list rather than presenting them separated by commas effectively stresses the individual components. Compare the following layouts:

The basic stages of development of insects are these: egg, larva, pupa, adult.

The basic stages of development of insects are these:
egg
larva
pupa
adult.

Similarly, adequate spacing between lines and the effective use of white space can contribute greatly to the clarity and impact of text. A consistent use of fonts, emphases, and layout patterns throughout your presentation will help greatly to make the content of your material easy for your readers to understand.

If your delivery medium is a computer screen, it is important to keep the placement of all screen elements consistent. Learners should always find directions, menus, areas for entering responses and so on in the expected location. (A corollary to this point is that students' actions with keyboard or mouse should always produce a consistent result.)

A further useful step in making decisions about text information may be using a readability index formula to assess the match of your presented text to the reading levels of your intended audience. Many word processing programs contain among their tools the option of calculating readability level. In general, it is wiser to write text at a readability level well within the expected range of your audience, and to focus on clarity and communication rather than style.

Let us remind ourselves at this point that discussing *writing* frames definitely does not mean that information must be limited to text: graphics, diagrams, mathematical or symbolic data can elicit responses, often better than words can do. But whatever the format of the data, it must be grouped into brief, coherent units, each of which elicits a meaningful response, all of which build together toward the desired outcome.

Visual elements such as pictures, diagrams, charts, graphs and various symbols are powerful communication tools for all aspects of expository instruction: presenting information, giving the learner guidance, setting up practice activities. Even assessing learning can sometimes be done through the use of visuals, either constructed or selected. You could ask learners to "draw a diagram of the circuit" or a similar kind of criterion question employing the use of graphics in the requested response.

When planning graphics for communication, we need to be aware of the effects of several graphic elements. Color is one such element. In simple graphics, color can add focus or emphasis. However, too much color or color used without attention to its effects can distract and interfere with communication. Even in familiar full-color formats such as video, color choice for backgrounds, for people's clothing, and even for minor objects in a given scene can either help or hinder the intended message.

Similarly, the level of detail or the degree of realism in a visual is an important consideration. Research suggests that a middle range of realism best conveys information. Presenting the critical attributes of the object represented and suppressing other non-essential parts helps learners focus on those attributes that need to be learned. Careful combination of graphics with text can help greatly to present

Effect of Levels of Realism

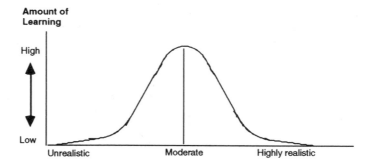

needed information clearly and completely, and in a form that will give rise to thoughtful processing of the information as the learners respond to it (Fleming, 1987).

Finally, "Active responding" must mean more than "press return to go on" or "turn to the next page." (Once in a while a direction to "go on to the next" may be necessary to allow information to be developed more extensively before the response, but it is wise to remember that the use of small steps is a basic principle of developing a really interactive tutorial.) Real learner interaction with the material is essential to good self-instruction. Thinking up the response request is the key skill in designing interactive learning.

Immediate feedback

The principle of immediate feedback also indicates that every response must produce a result. A correct answer to a question must be affirmed, though often it is sufficient that a correct response permits the learner to proceed, sometime simply by saying "Right" or "Okay" and presenting the next information block.

An error should be identified and remediated. With an incorrect or inappropriate response, learners are moved to a re-explanation or clarification of the misunderstood point and offered a second opportunity to respond. It is important that remediation should take learners to a new frame, not ask them to "go back and try again." Going backwards is a very aversive experience psychologically: further, if the idea was not clear to begin with, there is little point in simply revisiting it. If the response offered was a multiple choice question, learners can simply eliminate alternatives without necessarily improving understanding at all. In computer-based materials, a display can be held on the screen and clarifying changes made before the re-try response is asked for.

Wording for correction and remediation needs to be frank but positive, and should encourage learners to make the effort to understand. Try phrasing such as "Let's look at that another way," or "Here's is a different example that may help."

Sometimes the response carries its own feedback. Computer materials can display a comment or a correction when a button or area is clicked. Dragged items can be accepted, or rejected if incorrect by the program. But every response must produce a result if the important principle of "immediate feedback" is to be followed.

Sequencing

You may find that the familiar process of writing an outline for your content gets you started. From the outline you should be able to identify the concepts and/or rules that learners need to know about and the steps they must perform in a task. Your planning pyramid will suggest the essential sequence for presenting and explaining this information.

Usually a series of frames is necessary to build learners' understanding toward a level that makes possible a correct or appropriate response to the core ideas to be learned. In the expository approach, the presenting and guiding stages for each main idea typically move learners forward with gradually lessening guidance to the point at which they are ready to practice and apply the current content. At the conclusion of the series, the learner is ready for the criterion question or action you decided upon at the outset as the assessment of attainment of the objective.

A series of shorter frames with more active responding is ordinarily a better choice than a frame with a great deal of information It may be helpful to imagine that the text will be displayed on a computer screen, and to present information in increments that will fit that space. As we noted earlier, with current computer systems inclusion of segments of motion and sound are increasingly possible. With such capabilities, the concept of "small steps" includes not only space but time in the need for coherence, unity and focus. Location and layout remain as equally important considerations for these high-end systems.

With delivery formats such as web-based materials that provide the capability of linking numerous blocks of information, the issues of careful organizing of paths and connections becomes even more important. Some conventions are developing in this rapidly changing delivery mode: certain colors may indicate words which act as links, for example, and the necessity of assuring learners guidance for return or logical continuation is raising some entirely new design and format concerns. Perhaps we need to add "range" to space and time as issues in maintaining coherence. We will explore these ideas further as we investigate inquiry-based instruction. At this point let us remind ourselves that instruction as we are using the term implies a purposeful and partnered enterprise between designer, learner and material.

Spiral learning

Deciding the sequence of the frames offers varied opportunities for guiding learners toward the desired outcome. It often seems logical simply to begin at the beginning and plug straight along through to the end. However, it may be better to consider the style termed "spiral learning," in which a coherent group of concepts or steps is taught, followed by a second round of ideas and actions which expand on the basic set first presented.

An example might be the teaching of word processing to novices. Most manuals and many software tutorials group together all the information on each aspect of the program: all the formatting techniques, all the editing techniques, all the printing information and so on. A spiral approach would instead have an introductory experience in which the learner types in text, makes one or two minor editing changes, such as inserting or deleting a word, and then learns how to save the text as a file for later transfer. Such an experience is unified and satisfying: the learner feels she got somewhere. She is now ready to undertake the other processes available for entering, editing, and transferring text in increasingly more complex combinations.

Guidance and practice

For self-instruction to be effective, the learner must keep moving through the material: with no outside encouragement or assistance, it is necessary that the learners' own interest and motivation remain high to assure that they do indeed keep moving. If they are finding the learning experience successful, they are likely to do so. It is therefore important that the start of each sequence of interaction provide an initial sense of success.

Besides providing the easiest steps at first, we can present material in a format that facilitates understanding, as we shall explore more fully in a moment, and we can provide optional help or hints that learners may request if they wish. Research indicates that being able to acquire additional information at the time the need for it is identified helps motivate continued investigation and learning. (See Schank and Jona, 1991). This "just-in-time" assistance can be provided either by directly offering a choice— "Would you like more information? Press H" or "turn to page x"— or by responding to a faulty response with explanation and correction before returning the learner to the flow of information.

Prompting

To help guide the learner we may employ techniques termed "prompting." Prompting can be thought of as the clues or hints which increase the likelihood of the construction or selection of the correct or appropriate response. Techniques of prompting have been developed by designers of traditional forms of self-instruction which can often be usefully employed in even the most high-tech of today's delivery systems. Chief among these techniques is the careful choice of wording to suggest associations or connection with the desired response which learners may already have in place. An example of such a "thematic prompt" is seen here:

> Your telephone is one of your most important business tools. If the main advantage of the telephone is that it keeps you in touch with people you <u>want</u> to talk to, what is its main disadvantage?

Such an example builds on established associations among opposites for speakers of

English. Prompts can be done graphically as well. Look at the following example.

One basic rule of perspective is that "things appear bigger when they are close to us and smaller when they are farther away." Try this yourself. In the space below, draw one big ball and one little one, using the dots as their centers.

•   •

The little one looks as if it might be _____

_____.

(Or, "Which one looks further away?")

Developing a good tutorial requires the application of the basic principles of self-instruction through all the stages of expository instruction: the material must be in small enough steps to promote active responding as the information is presented. Responses must receive immediate feedback to guide learners and help them practice. The choices that each person makes move him through the material at the pace that works best for that individual, bringing each to the assessment frames ready for successful demonstration of the learning which has taken place.

Representing the design plan

Flow charts

To manage and keep track of the flow of the information we are working with, let's consider at this point some techniques for representing our devloping ideas. How can we go about getting our ideas from plans and preliminaries to a form from which the ideas can be implemented? A basic planning tool that can be very useful is flow charting.

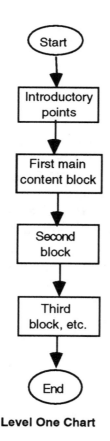

Level One Chart

Flow charts for progression through an expository lesson are generally straightforward. Alessi and Trollip (1991) suggest preparing a flow chart representation of your material in stages. Start with a simple diagram of your main blocks of content, as shown. This process will help you to determine what are the related knowledge and skills which naturally constitute a coherent and meaningful unit of your content material. Such a chart helps you answer the question, "What are we going to cover in this learning experience?" The basic flow chart symbols shown here are the ellipse, indicating the start and end of a sequence, and the rectangles, indicating the nature of the content.

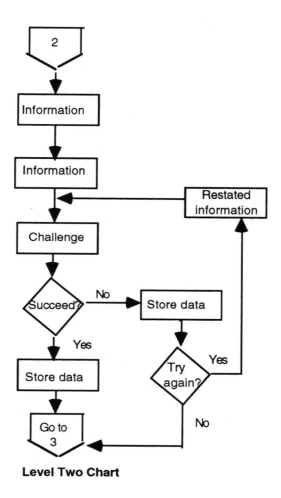

Level Two Chart

To develop more detailed representation we will need symbols to indicate points of interactions and the directions that decisions made at these points will take, as well the conventional symbols indicating connections between sections of the chart. A sample diagram of a path with decisions is shown.

The diamond is the decision indicator, and the connector to another section of the chart is shown at the beginning and ending of the sequence. Arrows show the direction of the flow of the program between its elements. More detailed representation of complex sections of your plan are possible beyond this second stage flow chart but not always necessary. Developing at least a functioning level of skill with basic, standard flow chart style can be a useful accomplishment for anyone involved with designing and developing instruction. A number of software programs exist to help with this process.

Scripting

With an overall plan laid out in flow chart form, you are now ready to develop the details of content and presentation more fully. A basic script for each of the principal blocks of information can be laid out in a two-column format. Verbal information-- text for written material, narration for audio, or guidelines and suggested wording for facilitators of live situations --is presented in one column, typically the right hand column, often with comments or directions to help the development of the non-verbal material which will be organized in the other column. Descriptions or sketches of visual material or actions are presented in the left-hand column. Often developing a script is the intermediate step between the planning level of the flow charts and the more detailed work of preparing a clear picture of each particular element of your material.

Story boarding

A story board is the visual representation of each significant block of information in your material which will guide the final stages of development of your material. Typically, separate cards or pages are used by designers to enable flexibility in sequencing the layout of the steps in the plan. Often a numbering or coding scheme is helpful to finalize the sequence and to indicate the flow of the presentation. Many suggested story-board formats are available as guides. For your own planning efforts, decide what works best for you, choosing or modifying as most effective for your own circumstances.

Again, the delivery medium you are working with will dictate some aspects of your choice. In any medium, we need to remember that small steps of material are a core design principle for self-instruction. Imagine your deliv-

Example Story Board Card 1

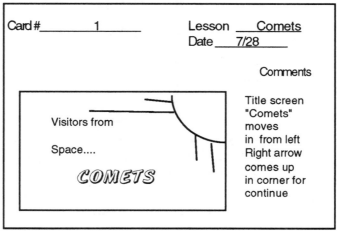

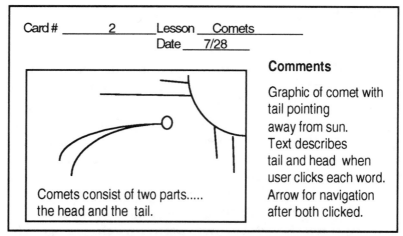

Card # _____2_____ Lesson ___Comets_____
                        Date ____7/28____

Comments

Comets consist of two parts.....
the head and the tail.

Graphic of comet with
tail pointing
away from sun.
Text describes
tail and head when
user clicks each word.
Arrow for navigation
after both clicked.

Example Story Board Card 2

ery format —page, screen, block of time— and lay out the necessary elements in the story board format that you select to guide the final actual development of your instruction , either for your own personal production or to communicate to others working with you to develop a product.

Student Testing: Formative Evaluation.

Planning and preparing your material is clearly a considerable investment of time and effort. Often, the self-instructional end product will be used by people we may never see with results we will never know: how can we tell whether all this work is successful and worth all the effort? It is here that the legacy of programmed instruction, the principle of student testing, can be invaluable.

PRINCIPLES OF SELF-INSTRUCTION
Active responding Immediate feedback Small steps Self-pacing
Student testing of materials

Formative evaluation, as the process is usually called, allows sample learners to try out the material as soon as it is sufficiently complete. You can also have sample learners try out an extensive project a section at a time during development.

Although more than one tester is desirable, at least one tester is almost mandatory. The process of "student testing" begins as soon as a reasonably complete first draft of your material exists. Plan this test carefully. Determine what you are looking for, what you reasonably expect to see happen, and note the points in your material about which may have any hesitation or uncertainty.

Make yourself a careful check list, section by section, and devise a way to record your sample learner's responses and reactions to each element you want to check out. Then give the material to your sample learner and ask her to read *out loud* while working through it. Explain that you want her to verbalize all her reactions as she goes: when she forms a mental question, she is to ask it out loud; as she makes a decision about what to do next, she is requested to say what she is thinking about as she determines each step.

You sit across the table as she works, or watch the terminal over her shoulder, listening carefully, keeping track with your check list of items, taking notes where your initial plan needs expanding. Sometimes it is useful to tape the procedure, either with video or audio, depending on the nature of the material and the circumstances and who else is involved in the design process.

You do not intervene with explanations or assistance even if asked to unless such action is essential to continue the trial run past the problem point. You hope that there will be few such major glitches, but it will be a rare test run if you do not find numerous smaller points of confusion, ambiguity or unexpected responses. . . which is exactly what we are looking for when we apply this important principle.

Sometimes it is possible to do a second trial run with another student tester after the revisions indicated by the first trial are made. Sometimes it may be necessary to do so, and sometimes it may be impossible to do so, but at least one serious checkout of the design is the best investment we can make in its success. Your careful record of the test run experience helps you assure that future learners have the benefit of this interaction between the materials, the learner, and you, the designer.

Summary

Expository instruction in the form of self-instructional materials presents numerous challenges to the designer. This format casts the instructional material in the role of the teacher or tutor and requires that the information presented, the responses and interactions expected, and the feedback provided should all accomplish the kind of communication which occurs when a good, direct teacher works with learners.

Some of the strengths of expository instruction available to a classroom teacher are simply not present in self-instructional settings: the opportunity to read student expressions, body language, tone of voice, to interpret the underlying meaning in questions, to call on the interpersonal skills of teaching are not available.

However, some of the limitations of classroom instruction are eliminated, such as the inability to pay adequate attention to each student in a large class, and the lack of time to explore and follow-up students' expressed interests in a variety of issues in a topic. In designing good tutorials, the instructional designer must balance the range of considerations and apply the range of principles, skills and techniques which we have discussed in this section of this book.

With these steps taken, you should have an instructional product that represents the application of the many elements we have looked at thus far. The implied contract between the learner and the designer can be fulfilled, and the satisfying experience of successful learning will occur for those learners as the outcome of your efforts as your designer.

A look ahead

An expository model of self-instruction, as we have seen, presents information and asks guiding questions. When well-done, expository instruction models the process of developing questions for the learner and can also offer learners the opportunity to ask questions through various techniques. We will look in the following section of this book at the delivery style which focuses upon learner inquiry as the means for interacting with the body of information which we want our instruction to "make different,......to facilitate learning."

REFERENCES AND SUGGESTIONS FOR FURTHER READING.

Alessi, S. M., & Trollip, S. R. (1991). Computer-based instruction: Methods and development. (2nd ed.). Englewood Cliffs, NJ: Prentice Hall.

Bloom, B. S. (1984). The 2 sigma problem: The search for methods of group instruction as effective as one-to-one tutoring. Educational Researcher, 6, 4-16.

Deutsch, W. (1992). Teaching machines, programming, computers, and instructional technology: The roots of performance technology. Performance & Instruction, 31 (2), 14-20.

Fleming, M. L. (1987). Displays and communication. In Gagne, R. M.(Ed.). Instructional Technology: Foundations. Englewood Cliffs, NJ: Erlbaum.

Gagne, R. (1985). Conditions of learning. (4th edition). New York: Holt, Rinehart & Winston.

Kemp, J. E. (1985). The instructional design process. New York: Harper & Row.

Knirk, F. G. & Gustafson, K. L. (1986). Instructional technology: A systematic approach to education. New York: CBS College Publishing.

Mager, R. F. (1984). Preparing instructional objectives. (2nd ed.). Belmont, CA: Lake.

Mager, R. F. (1991). Norman Crowder. Update, 11, Carefree, AZ: Mager Associates.

Markle, S. M. (1964). Good frames and bad. New York: Wiley.

Markle, S. M. (1981). Designs for instructional designers. Champaign, IL: Stipes.

Niemec, R. P., & Walberg, H. J. (1989). From teaching machines to microcomputers: Some milestones in the history of computer-based instruction. Journal of Research on Computing in Education, 21, 263-276.

Pipe, P. (1966). Practical programming. New York: Holt, Rinehart & Winston.

Piskurich, G. M. (1991). Ensure Quality and quality training through self-directed learning. Training and Development Journal, 45, 37-38.

Piskurich, G. M. (1993). Self-directed learning. San Francisco: Jossey-Bass.

Rosenshine, B. (1983). Teaching functions in instructional programs. Elementary School Journal, 83 (4), pp. 335-351.

Schank, R. C., & Jona, M. Y. (1991). Empowering the student: New perspectives on the design of teaching systems. Journal of Learning Sciences, 1, 7-35.

Skinner, B. F. (1986). Programmed instruction revisited. Phi Delta Kappan, October, 103-110.

Chapter Three: Inquiry-based Self-Instruction

In the following section of this book we will consider the design and development of instruction for delivery in the form variously referred to as inquiry-based learning, discovery learning, or experiential learning. We look in this style at a shift from an emphasis on telling by the tutor to asking by the learner. Let us begin with a brief exploration of the theoretical and philosophical background for this kind of instruction, and then move on to consideration of some ways and means to design and develop self-instructional learning experiences which will make effective use of our most current understanding of human learning.

Theoretical background

Throughout history, the teachers, trainers, coaches, educators of all kinds who have been entrusted with determining how to convey content to learners have always been practicing instructional designers. Psychological science in the last hundred years or so has presented various theories to explain how and why learning occurs when such expert practitioners interact effectively with novices: what do these experts know and do, and how do they convey their expertise to learners?

As we noted to begin with, early learning theorists focused on changes in people's actions, their behaviors, as indications of changes in their knowledge and skills, that is, as indications of what they had learned from being taught about a topic or how to do a task. We considered at some length the tradition of behavioral psychology and its effect on such forms of self-instruction as programmed learning. From the very beginning of this book, we have emphasized the idea of mental or cognitive "behavior" change as the necessary bridge between observable actions and the internal, truly significant outcome in learning situations.

Away from Behaviorism

The shift from the behaviorist view of changes in performance to the cognitivist view of changes in mental competencies as indications of learning has been the subject of extensive research. Recent years have seen the rise of a school of thought known as "constructivism," which maintains that learners must build their understanding of their world though experience, that knowledge and skill are constructed by each individual through his or her own interactions with the environment. (This position is not altogether new to education:

the developmental theories of Jean Piaget and pragmatism, John Dewey's belief in "learning by doing," are familiar to school based educators.)

The constructivist view that learning is "a change in the meaning of experience" presents some problems to a designer who must attempt to provide learners with the experiences through which they will construct and change their perception of the meaning of that experience. The core issue here must be a serious consideration of the extent to which the instructional designer "expert" must contribute to the available experience, and the extent to which the "novice" must identify and respond to his perceptions of his "need to know." What outcomes of such experience will appropriately and effectively match the world outside the learning situation?

A thoughtful and responsible commitment from providers of learning experiences must be matched in this philosophy by a thoughtful and responsible involvement from learners if meaningful change is indeed to take place. Developing such a commitment to learning has implications for all adults who interact with children, and for schools, the structures which society provides for children's formal learning, and for all learners as they mature sufficiently to direct their learning more independently.

Schema theory

The information which people acquire through their experiences we can say is "learned" when it is stored and accessible for recall from memory. Researchers have developed various descriptions of the way learned information is stored and accessed.

One useful representation of how information is organized in long-term memory is the concept of the "schema." A schema is the person's organized set of knowledge about a particular experience. There is an element of story or script to the idea of the schema, the narrative we make about the ideas contained in the schema. What you know about writing a paper for class or performing some part of your job is organized in your memory partly as the things you know *about* paper writing or your job, and partly as what you know *how* to do to accomplish the writing of the paper or the performance of the job. There is also an element of mental pictures or mental models for components of your overall organizing schema (Paivio, 1979).

An oversimplification of the concept of the schema which may be helpful is the idea of a schema as an expandable file folder with various slots. Learning may add content to a given slot, group the content of various slots together into one bigger slot, or even add a new slot entirely. There are more scholarly and detailed ways to represent the connections between and among the components of information we store, but for our purposes the schema as a container may work.

Every person will have an individual schema for a concept or topic, with variations among the details which compose it. However, we do seem to develop certain broad commonalties of understanding for the ideas encountered in our society, and that is why within a given society we can usually largely understand one another's "meanings." We may group up different component details for an idea, but the overall, integrated concept represents many shared or similar experiences. It is this emphasis on the meaningful integration of elements of experience which strongly influences some of the theories for designing learning experiences which we will explore next.

Phases of Experiential Learning

As we considered expository instruction, we dealt with the four phases of instruction suggested by Alessi and Trollip (1991) as an expository model. Let us look now at how this basic underlying model of instruction is altered when we consider an inquiry-based, experiential learning model. The idea does not change radically in form, but it definitely changes significantly in its focus and in its implications for instructional design. Let's put them side by side:

PHASES OF INSTRUCTION EXPOSITORY LEARNING MODEL (Alessi & Trollip)	PHASES OF INSTRUCTION EXPERIENTIAL LEARNING MODEL (Keirns)
Presenting information	Providing information
Guiding the student	Coaching, advising the student
Practicing by the student	Experiencing by the student
Assessing student learning	Student monitoring of progress

Expository-Experiential Models Contrasted

When we think of the content of a lesson as information *presented* to students, there is an obvious necessity for the designer/tutor to structure the presentation carefully with a view to assuring that the student will be appropriately guided through it. When we think of the content of a lesson as information provided to the student through which he or she selects the path, a change occurs in how we view the content itself.

If we are *providing* information, the first thing we must do is to assure that coherent blocks of content are accessible to the learners: since we are backing off from guiding the learner along a particular path, we must be sure that the paths provided for learner exploration are clear, complete, and related to one another.

We can conceive of content organized not only in sequential blocks along a route but in layers of information, a kind of three-dimensional model. Instead of branching off to the side, so to speak, learners can dig deeper into a particular block of information to explore and build personal meaning, while yet not losing a meaningful sequence of experiences leading to the desired basic understanding of the content.

Three Dimensional Flow of Information

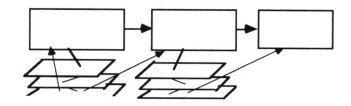

Formats for experiential learning

Broadly speaking, the most widely used format for providing information which learners can explore and interact with is termed "simulation." By this we mean that designers provide information embodied in scenarios, stories related to real life, within which learners can generate questions, propose and test hypotheses about alternate courses of action, and acquire information about the consequences of various choices in the given setting, in a way which imitates or simulates our functioning in real life.

Simulations can provide information about physical laws and principles, allowing learners to manipulate, predict, and calculate results of interactions among natural phenomena. Many kinds of physical, social, and natural processes can be simulated, with the benefit of allowing the time needed to observe the outcomes of the process to be either speeded up or slowed down as appropriate. Similarly, procedures requiring the learning of various steps and the making of decisions at certain points can be simulated, permitting learners to troubleshoot or predict events within the simulated system.

Situational simulations have been used in many fields for many years. Such simulations provide a context in which learners assume and act out roles, observing the constraints which the simulated situation imposes and acting upon the opportunities which it affords. Examples range from the Lemonade Stand game on the early Apple computer to the mock legislature in Civics class. Business and industry use both situational simulations and the closely related game format for certain kinds of training.

What makes simulations work

The elements which make simulations effective include the factors which make self-instruction in general effective. Learners are very actively involved in a simulation, the nature of the setting is such that learner choice provides the immediate feedback of a consequence, and a simulation is highly self-directed, whether undertaken by an individual or a group. Simulations offer the strength of providing a more nearly "authentic" experience than many other kinds of instruction, giving learners a sense of what real-world activity with the content involves. Placing learning in a context helps develop what researchers have termed "situated cognition" or "cognitive apprenticeship" (Brown, Collins, & Duguid, 1989; Collins, Brown, & Newman, 1989.)

Designing Inquiry-based Instruction: Fundamental Considerations

The planning and designing stages for inquiry-based, experiential self-instruction are similar to the design stage for all kinds of instruction, but there are several ways in which such design is different. The processes for analyzing learning needs which we considered for expository instruction tended to rely on breaking tasks or topics down into steps or components or elements. Determining objectives for the learners was an initial step: we began by identifying outcomes considered both as cognitive and observable performances. The information to be presented, the skills to be practiced, the assessments to be offered arose from this careful process. We looked at each expected skill step and considered what content was needed to help learners meet that objective.

We are now considering learning needs from a more integrative perspective. We are focusing on how the information content to be learned meshes with the things people do with that content, and on the various contexts in which these combinations of knowledge and skills have meaning and usefulness. In considering experiential learning, we can see the obvious emphasis on doing, the familiar performance objectives.

A central point of this book throughout, however, has been the emphasis on the cognitive performances that underlie observable actions. I see this emphasis as clustering knowledge and skills into abilities or *competencies* and will use this term as we move on to consider the design and development of inquiry based, experiential learning in simulation formats. Planning learning experiences in this manner requires a focus on identifying an overall, integrative representation of the competencies which we hope learners will arrive at.

Content

While content for simulations can come from almost any subject area, the selection of the actual material to be covered in the simulation will require a broader, more integrative identification of the topic than might be appropriate for a direct, expository lesson. A theme with a range of associated concepts and actions matches this kind of design.

Schank (1993; 1996) uses the term "goal-based scenarios" to describe the overall context which makes an effective simulation. This is not to suggest that a simulation must be a very large or lengthy product, but to emphasize that the integration of components rather than concern with components separately must be the governing intent underlying the design plan. Fitting any worthwhile topic into a meaningful, scenario kind of context is the work of the designer of a simulation-type learning experience.

Learners

However, we need to be aware that some kinds of content are not efficiently taught in a simulation or experiential format, nor are all learners at ease with this type of learning experience. The decision to invest the considerable time and effort to develop instruction in this format must rest upon a thoughtful analysis of the content to be taught, the learning situation, and the learners themselves.

Learners are directly responsible for many more aspects of their interaction with the content in this setting than was the case with the typical expository, tutorial lesson we considered earlier. The designer must provide more kinds of choices to allow for the varying experiences which the learners bring to the instructional setting in which they will be constructing new schemas or extending, modifying or elaborating existing schemas. Frequently, more than one path through the content to a desired outcome is possible, and there may also be a range of expressions for the desired outcome. How can we go about describing what learning outcomes students should reach in such a situation?

Variations on the Implied Contract

<u>Establishing learning goals</u>

We still need to state a goal and to identify the skills and knowledge that are associated with reaching that goal. Our first challenge is still to consider what learners will be able to do, both cognitively and in observable actions, when they have learned the content of the instruction. Here we can turn to the idea of "cognitive apprenticeship" mentioned earlier and consider what experts in our content area are able to do, what competencies they possess which enable them to act expertly. As noted earlier, we can think of these competencies as clusters of the skills and the knowledge that underlies them, which learners seek to attain.

What is the broadest definition for the "schema" or overall theme of the content we want to provide our learners? If the expert can "manage a classroom" or "develop a strategic business plan" or "troubleshoot equipment malfunction" or "conduct an expedition," we can see that there are many specific situations which would illustrate the application of the knowledge and skills that make up the competency of the expert applying that schema in the real world. It is readily apparent as well that there are many important, useful and interesting sub-competencies, each with its own components of knowledge and skill, which go into the overall goal.

Deciding on a scenario, an example situation or setting which illustrates the competency or group of competencies to be learned, is the next challenge. For many business or industry settings, a scenario closely representing the actual work situation is an obvious choice. School-related content may take more imagination, --and allow for more invention-- but the designer must provide some kind of meaningful story in which the end skills are to be practiced and the related knowledge to be applied in a coherent and plausible context. In both business and school settings, there should be room for a variety of appropriate results, and opportunity for a variety of approaches to reach the desired outcome.

Evaluating outcomes

Note also that in this kind of learning situation, there are likely to be a variety of "desired outcomes" as well. There can be more than one appropriate strategic business plan, more than one workable solution to the problem of getting an expedition through the rain forest. How then will learners assess whether they have indeed learned? As the Experiential Learning Model presented earlier indicates, here too the learner assumes more responsibility than in the Expository model. Learners must monitor their progress, assess the suitability of their choices in the light of the feedback from the simulation itself, and reflect on what alternate results they might have obtained from alternate choices. The designer will need to assure realistic and believable feedback to assist learners in this self-assessment role.

This is not to suggest that in experiential learning, anything goes. Mistakes and errors can occur in troubleshooting or conducting an expedition, and they have consequences. Misunderstandings, miscalculations and inaccuracies are not ignored by the developing scenario. But the learner is directly involved in the figuring out and the calculating, and will experience the results of trying to apply knowledge and to use developing skills in a believable context. The context gives meaning to the necessity for understanding, calculating, and making accurate use of data. The element of fantasy allows learners to investigate, inquire and try out: such questioning behavior leads to answers with real meaning, because they are arrived at and assessed by the learners themselves.

Evaluation in expository instruction focuses on criterion levels, and is often expressed in acceptable percentage levels. Evaluation in experiential instruction may also occasionally use "score" type information. "Give yourself ten points if you used the tools to build a raft, twenty points if you thought of using the crate lids to float the supplies across." Simulations resemble games in several aspects, and may borrow from games for assessment when appropriate for audience and content.

More commonly, learners may be expected to track and summarize their learning, comparing their results to "expert" choices presented for consideration, and determining their next choices accordingly. O'Neil and Baker (1993) and Jonassen (1995) have done some interesting work in assessment based on this comparison of expected "expert" performance with the performance of novice learners in various settings.

A main point about assessing learning in the experiential style is that outcomes are not viewed as the ends of instruction but as points along the way toward the increasingly greater competency which the learners can now apply in contexts outside the simulated learning environment.

Thus, at both ends of the implied contract there is a broadening of the essential concept: the intention of learning from interacting with the body of information in an experiential format must be present, but the nature of the intended learning is less constrained. Similarly, the necessary evaluation of the learning becomes part of the process of the experience rather than a separately assessed end. However, it remains the challenge of the designer to deal with the information content of this kind of self-instruction in such a way as to "make it different, to facilitate learning."

Planning Experiential Instruction: A Model

What models exist to help guide us in this non-traditional use of a new paradigm for learning and instructing? The familiar basic ID models remain broadly useful, but some recent modifications will be considered in this section of the book. For the moment, a useful "how-to" variation on the idea of Pipe's planning pyramid has been found by my students to offer direction in planning inquiry-based learning.

McGinn (1994) has developed a "Constructivist Instructional Design Model" upon which the following diagram is based. We will look later at the more detailed representation of some of the stages in this model.

This model, like the earlier Pyramid we considered, is essentially a top-down design tool. However, once a decision is made about the end competencies for the instruction, the designer may move through the components in the other levels along various paths. The first task is the selection of the comprehensive, integrative theme and end competencies which will allow the designer to consider the contexts and supporting skills and knowledge he or she will work with in developing the instructional experience.

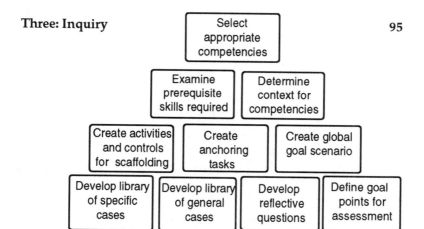

Constuctivist Instructional Design Model

<u>Selecting competencies</u>

When the end competency is clearly a skill, it is easier to state what integrative, overall ability we are trying to develop: "Provide effective consulting services to a new business;" "Produce a weekly school newspaper." When the overall theme is first seen as knowledge rather than skill, we need to do some thinking about what people *do* with this knowledge content. In what contexts and for what purposes do people use knowledge about "Primates?" or "Dinosaurs?" or "Renaissance painting?"

When learners are interested in a topic area, they will bring to bear such important and integrative skills as analyzing information, calculating, hypothesizing, composing and so on. An interesting context can provide a setting in which to "anchor" these skills to interesting and immediately meaningful outcomes. Thus, when we develop simulations or experiences about "primates" or "paintings", we are not aiming at having learners recall blocks of facts or be tested on example problems. The purpose of the experiential approach and the simulation format is to combine knowledge and skills in authentic, interesting task situations which will help learners to develop and apply significant end competencies that unite both knowledge and skill.

Our design plan, then, must look first at what competencies our learners wish and need to attain, and next at the possible contexts in which these competencies are exercised, and then at what prerequisite knowledge and skill must be present for learners to reach that competency. The block immediately below "examine prerequisites" identifies "scaffolding" as a means to address this concern. This important idea will be developed in the following paragraphs.

Determining Contexts

At this stage let us move down the right side of the model to consider the context for the learning experience we are designing, the setting for the simulation, the actions to be simulated, the environment in which we may place the content and interactions we intend to lead to the desired outcomes. Contexts for effective simulations need to be sufficiently complex to provide the range of possible interactions that we have seen are basic to this form. If, for example, our desired end competency is that learners will "be able to conduct effective negotiations," what kinds of arenas of human activity does this competency apply to? You can probably think of several immediately.

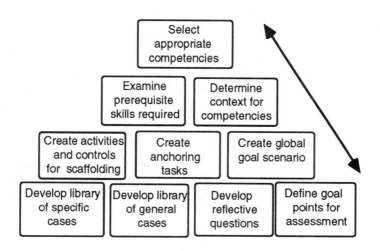

Moving down one more layer of the model in a moment, we can next turn our attention to inventing an interesting and content-rich global scenario, the actual setting for the activities and experiences of the simulation. Settling disputes in a classroom, establishing an agreement for a new business among the partners, hiring for-- or interviewing for-- a job might represent the overall story to be explored to illustrate the kind of context in which the desired competency of effective negotiating is applied. A good simulation provides a coherent and plausible overall setting. We will look presently at the step of developing several kinds of example cases which we may provide for learners to interact with.

Examining prerequisite skills

To move to the left side of the model, note that as you examine possible contexts, you will also need to consider what kinds of experiences learners must already have had in order to be ready to function in the contexts you are considering. For example, before people are ready to enter into any kind of negotiation, they must be able to express a point of view clearly, and be able to attend to what other people say. These experiences may have come from settings other than the context for the simulation, but they are necessary for learners to function in the context.

A major weak point in constructivism must be the question of what previous experience learners have on hand when they enter into the construction of new learning. Erroneous and flawed constructions may be a possible outcome of experience based on limited or inaccurate experiential data: while truth may not always be universal, there are certain commonalities of human interaction with the physical and social environment upon which we rely.

At this point we are ready to explore the further levels of the model and move to developing the instructional content of the simulation. We are ready to consider the concepts of "scaffolding" and "anchoring" as we begin to build the overall, global scenario for the learning experience.

IMPORTANT TO NOTE

It should be evident that planning instruction in this format is more time-consuming both for the designer and the learner than the expository, tutorial approach. In school settings, you are looking at interdisciplinary units more than content specific activities. In business or industry, you are dealing with topics like team building, or quality assurance rather than how to use new software. Obviously, determining which approach to take for a given instructional setting is one of the very first design considerations one must make: content and client needs must dictate your choice. Both type of self-instruction can be interesting and effective, building motivation and leading to achievement. Your overall designer skills will help you select the appropriate focus.

Developing Inquiry-based Instruction

As we have seen, there is not a definite line between design and development, but as our more general plan begins to take on specific points, we can say we are working on developing our instruction. We will be moving through several cycles as we think about producing our final product for self-instruction, and we will move back and forth among the blocks of our Model.

Applying the principles of self-instruction to simulations

Throughout this development stage, we are very directly and actively concerned with the principles which make self-instruction effective. The experiential, simulation format, even more than a good expository lesson, is centrally involved with active responding and immediate feedback in all the available interactions.

The shift in focus from expository to inquiry-based delivery means that the "active responding" now often takes the form of generating rather than answering questions. Frequent decision points and choices are the hallmark of the simulation, and every learner action produces a result; but sometimes the effect of these results may be cumulative and complex as the learner builds up a store of information from these decisions. You may need to be inventive in providing means for learners to track their actions in order to provide feedback and help them assess their understanding. Later we will consider later some possible tools and techniques to do this.

In this delivery style it remains true that a generally successful experience maintains interest and motivation, but a good simulation may allow a learner to fail to reach a goal. However, this kind of error can be experienced by the learner as successfully determining what does *not* work or fit with the goal if the actions and setting of the simulation are well-

designed and opportunity to try again is provided and made inviting. This view is again
somewhat different from the expository concept of remediation, because once again the focus is on the learner's generating of further
questions to ask rather than on the tutor's task
of identifying and correcting a mistake.

The levels of the Model we have considered
thus far are basically design or planning considerations. Let us begin our consideration of
development with the idea of the "global scenario" in the next level. This level will also
help us see what the concepts of "scaffolding
and "anchoring" imply in leading to experiences that will move learners toward the desired end competency. These considerations in
turn will clarify the model's components of
"specific cases" and "general cases" and give us
a grasp on the ideas of developing reflective
questioning and assessment points.

Creating a global scenario

We touched earlier on the idea of the global
scenario, the overall setting in which the
learning experiences are to be situated. Schank
(1996) gives examples of such scenarios, each of
which can embody many "cases" or illustrative
stories to involve the learner in making decisions, locating or generating data to apply
within the story setting, and information
about the results of such interactions. De Jong
and Mensink(1995) report the development
of computer-based training for law enforce-
ment students utilizing the global scenario ap-

proach. Similar use of scenario formats is described by Keegan (1993) for a wide variety of school topics. Let us look in greater detail at some examples of this format.

As an example, Schank describes a simulation called "Broadcast News" in which high school students act as producers of a newscast for a particular day in recent history. This context affords a broad interdisciplinary approach to history, geography, politics and economics, requiring the learner to think critically about the material provided in the form of a draft news story about the selected day, accompanying video and various reference sources as he develops what will be his personal format for the presentation of the information he gathers and analyzes. Clearly, a wide range of information and interactions is possible in such a global scenario.

Yordy (1991) describes a hypermedia program in which junior high students explore the broad topic of "Primates." The learning experience is cast in the global scenario of an interplanetary mission on which students help a scientist, the "Wiz," solve a series of problems requiring application of knowledge about primates. The necessary information is provided through various sources, including videodisc and information within the computer program itself.

The specific problem that Yordy presents as an example is the "Stowaway Monkey" problem, in which the Wiz requests students' help in returning to its proper habitat the monkey which he has discovered hiding on board his spaceship. Students must determine the critical characteristics of the monkey (several possible cases are included in the material) to determine its species and then identify the appropriate habitat to which the stowaway should be returned.

Schank's scenario example with the news broadcast is quite evidently aiming at developing observable skills applicable to a real-world setting. The "Primates Project," on the other hand, develops for school children the very important and broadly applicable skills of analyzing information, generalizing and discriminating among concepts, and predicting results of procedures and processes.

Theorists such as Gagne suggest that such skills are to some extent "domain-independent:" that is, such mental skills and cognitive strategies can be learned and utilized with information in all subject areas. Applying these skills in the subject area of the Primate Project leads learners to develop knowledge, conceptual understanding and awareness of principles and processes related to humans, apes, monkeys and their interactions with their environments.

The approach of the simulation helps learners construct these understandings through their experiences with the information rather than steering them to such understanding by *receiving* and practicing with the information. Both expository and experiential delivery styles can lead to development of this kind of knowledge and identified skills, but the more involved the learner, the more meaningful and thus memorable such knowledge and skills are likely to be.

In applying this idea of the complex scenario, my students have placed fifth-grade learners in the role of fire safety inspector, charged with developing a neighborhood fire safety program; teen-agers have been given the role of being responsible for managing and budgeting job and allowance income to meet selected goals; and for adults a wide range of roles have been designed, from acting as historian for a religious denomination to serving as substitute foreman on an ostrich ranch. In these scenarios, too, it is possible to develop numerous specific situations to explore and to provide a great variety of interactions for the learner with the information content which will provide opportunity to attain and apply the desired end competency.

Taking all these ideas into consideration, we could describe an effective scenario for a simulation as having the components presented in the box on the following page. The concept of the "global scenario" in our Model deals with the first three of these components. As we look at "situations," we will be moving on through other elements of the Model.

```
┌─────────────────────────────────────────────────────────┐
│  COMPONENTS OF AN EFFECTIVE GOAL-BASED SCENARIO          │
│        FOR A SIMULATION      (After Schank, 1993)        │
│                                                          │
│  CONTEXT:        Statement of what we are going to undertake│
│  THE "MISSION"   to accomplish that will demonstrate application│
│                  of the named end competency being sought│
│                                                          │
│  THE "COVER      An engaging and coherent narrative      │
│  STORY"          description of the context in which the mission│
│                  is to be carried out                    │
│                                                          │
│  LEARNER'S       A plausible and desirable part to play through│
│  ROLE: THE       which the individual interacts with the │
│  ANCHORING       information content of the Cover Story in order│
│  TASKS           to achieve the Mission goal             │
│                                                          │
│  SITUATIONS:     The specific events and activities in the│
│  SPECIFIC        simulation which provide the means for the│
│  CASES           learner to interact with the information content│
│                  of the Cover Story to develop the target│
│                  competencies                            │
└─────────────────────────────────────────────────────────┘
```

Anchoring tasks

In the center of the third row of the Model we find the block identifying the need to "Create Anchoring Tasks." This term refers to the activities in which learners engage in order to apply to specific situations the appropriate knowledge and skill embodied in the end competency we are aiming for. We have used as examples of global scenarios the production of a news broadcast, solving "primate problems," and conducting various kinds of negotiations: the anchoring tasks within these selected scenarios might be represented by editing a draft news story to provide clearer background information about a given event, by identifying the stowaway monkey's species as

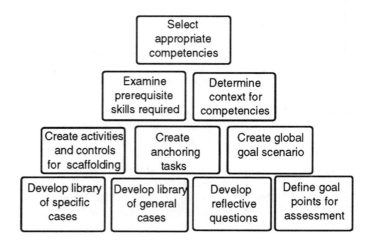

mentioned earlier, or by developing a step by step plan for the negotiations involved in your job interview with the particular company described in the cover story of the scenario.

An important aspect of the idea of an anchored task is that it is a *representative* application: if learners can successfully edit a particular story, identify a given monkey, or interview for a specified position, the knowledge and skills used in this specific task have developed toward being transferable to other stories, other monkeys, other interviews. The concept of the anchored task expands the concept of "practicing by the student" from the more focused expository learning situation to a more generic view of the meaning of the learning experience.

An Example of Anchored Instruction

A widely cited and interesting project involving the concept of anchored instruction is the "Jasper Woodbury" series of videodisc materials developed by the Cognition and Technology Group at Vanderbilt University. Jasper's adventures provide learners the opportunity to formulate and solve a wide range of mathematical problems arising from the story information. (Related materials including information data bases permit the Jasper stories to be tied to other content areas such as history, geography, weather, etc.) Students must recognize the nature of a problem situation, formulate a means to solve it, and locate the pertinent data from the events and details of the story, thus "anchoring" mathematical skills in a meaningful and believable context.

For example, Jasper must return to his home dock by sunset from a day trip in his motor boat. Students must recognize the main problem of "Can he reach home from where he is in the remaining time?" and also the sub-problems of "Just how far must he go?" "Does he have enough gas to cover that distance?" "How long is it until sunset?"

All the data necessary to formulate and answer these questions is present in the video: Jasper's map can be reviewed, the radio broadcasts of daily marine information can be replayed, the clock and gas gauge can be rechecked and so on. Forming such questions and applying mathematical knowledge to solve them gives real, everyday meaning to the concepts of distance, rate and time, a far more engaging learning experience than the "example word problems" that may come to your mind for those concepts.

The term "anchored instruction" used by this group of researchers at Vanderbilt and the term "situated cognition" or "cognitive apprenticeship" used by Brown, Collins, Duguid, Newman and their associates all emphasize the "authentic" nature of addressing the learning experiences of identifying problems, locating or generating necessary data, proposing and testing various solution processes, and making and evaluating decisions, as people need to do in real life settings.

In line with this thinking, schools have recently moved toward "authentic assessment" practices in many areas, asking students to deal with real problems, and produce real products rather than being evaluated on sample questions outside of any meaningful context, to assess attainment of knowledge and skill.

Developing instruction in the simulation format which we are exploring is one way that schools, business and industry can provide such meaningful contexts for either groups or individual learners to demonstrate desired skills and apply associated knowledge. Thus, our effort in determining appropriately complex and interesting global scenarios leads directly to our opportunities to create engaging anchoring tasks for the learning experience.

Scaffolding

As we considered the necessity to identify areas of prerequisite knowledge and skill for a given learning situation, we touched upon the idea of scaffolding, which we will now explore further. We have observed that an issue with a constructivist viewpoint must be the problem of insufficient or inaccurate previous experience which learners may bring to a new situation, giving them insufficient knowledge or skill to begin the learning experience effectively and raising the possibility of inadequate or unworkable constructions.

The concept of scaffolding provides a means for the designer to help the learner acquire either missing knowledge or skill before undertaking the tasks which require them. The designer must offer, or actively assure, interactions which enable the learner to develop or apply such prerequisite competency, just as a real-life master of apprentices would select a variety of tasks for novices, based upon his expert observation and assessment of each novice's skills and knowledge as he enters and continues his apprenticeship training.

Levels

One approach is to develop a simulation scenario structured, as many interactive games are, on "levels." A game player may not play an "expert" level game until he has scored an expert level score on earlier tries. Similarly, a newscast producer or negotiator may be required by the structure of the simulation to succeed at tasks at the prerequisite skill level before undertaking the more complex tasks of the scenario. The reporter begins with responsibilities for re-writing news wire information, then covers events in the field, finally developing the commentary section of the broadcast.

This approach is a kind of "remediation in advance" which can allow a learner to explore information, form and test hypotheses while still avoiding the wasted experience of blind guesses or actions taken without sufficient understanding of the context to be the kind of meaningful choices which build learning.

"Help" interactions

Another technique of scaffolding is even more broadly applicable to provide learners the support and assistance they need to build new learning on a solid foundation. This technique is the provision of extensive opportunities for learner-initiated "help" interactions.

Merrill (1988) mentions several useful "help" options which can be made available either as stated choices at interaction points or as options always available from a special "help" menu, such as: "Show me a...map, diagram, chart, graph, picture; a rule, a definition, an explanation; an example, an easier example, a harder example,: tell me how I am doing, suggest what would be a good step to take next." Other kinds of help interactions might include the availability of a calculator or similar tool

	HELP INTERACTIONS
Show me	map, diagram, chart, graph, picture
Give me	rule, definition, example (easier, harder), another problem
Tell me	how I am doing so far, what would be a good step to take next
Provide me	a tool (dictionary, calculator, record book)

devices, or the "hot text" which some kinds of soft-ware provide for defini-tions, explan-ations or ex-tensions of selected words or phrases.

However, these kinds of available "help" sections do not have to be on-line, computer- based interactions. Imagine, for example, a self-study booklet to go home with attendees between sessions at a two-day workshop. A standard self-instructional kind of presentation of frames of material could be augmented with color-coding of terms which might be unfamil-iar: a color-coded section at the back of the booklet could readily be checked for the "blue" words on various pages, or red coded informa-tion could trigger an investigation of the red section of the booklet for supporting "help" material of various kinds. Any imaginative means to make optional, supportive material available to the learner would qualify as this kind of scaffolding help, allowing learners to progress at the pace which matches their needs, applying the principle of self-pacing in an experiential delivery format just as we did in an expository style.

Applying the concept of scaffolding

An example may help clarify the scaffolding concept. In a simulation dealing with content in which prerequisite knowledge includes particular vocabulary, such as an expedition through the rain forest or to study a volcanic region, an early interaction might consist of the request by the expedition leader that the learner assist in preparing a "dictionary" for new recruits. The learner's job would be to pair up essential terms and their definitions or illustrations for the hypothetical recruit, thereby, of course, assuring that the learner correctly understands or learns them by investigating any he is not sure of. The developed "dictionary" could then serve as a tool or resource as the learner progresses through the simulation. Similar kinds of entering activities can be invented to position learners with other kinds of necessary knowledge or skill before they embark on the main experiences of the simulation.

Developing situations for interactions: Specific cases, general cases

At this final level of development, we are ready to design the "small steps" of specific interactions with scenario content which constitute the actual experiences of the simulation. Here we develop the cover story into the actions and decisions through which the learner builds his knowledge and skill. "The interviewer gives you a list of the main duties of the position you are applying for. He asks you to check the two you believe you are best at, and one you may feel you need to learn more about. What do you check?" An example list is presented, the learner makes decisions, the simulation records them, and feedback information is developed.

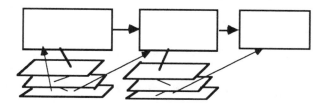

"Layers" of Information

At these interaction points we see the layered blocks of information diagrammed earlier coming into play. The learner may request more information as "help" type interactions, returning to the main flow when ready after digging as far down as necessary through the layers of content. Or he or she may move directly to a decision and initiate the next interaction that will result from that choice.

An interesting and realistic story line will typically offer a variety of possible choices, thus a variety of possible outcomes, and the designer is therefore faced with the need to consider careful development of many interacting and inter-related experiences for the learner to work with. We will consider a bit later some techniques to keep track of the probably complex flow of such actions.

General Cases

The distinction made in the Model between a library of specific cases and a library of general cases addresses the need to back up the specific story line of the simulation with the more general example cases which learners may need to access to clarify their particular choice. Cases which present a general illustration of a rule or principle may be needed to clarify choices to be made in a specific setting that is an example of the functioning of the rule or principle.

For example, to help in editing the particular news story presented by the simulation, the learner might select an option to have an expert editor give some advice about tricks and techniques for analyzing news stories in general. The kinds of specific and/or general cases appropriate to a given scenario will of course vary greatly. The point here is that these "cases" are the situations that make up the activities and build the experiences by means of which our simulation is to help the learner arrive at the desired competencies.

Reflective questions and assessment points

The remaining blocks in our Model are the ones that represent the fulfillment aspect of the implied contract of self-instruction. Just as the paths through the learning experience have been more learner-directed in this style of delivery, so is the assessment of the outcomes more learner-directed.

It is the role of the designer to assure the learner the necessary opportunities to evaluate progress toward the intended goals of the simulation. This will require that at logical intervals, the action afforded by the situation will provide a kind of "indicator" outcome. If the learner has been working with developing a plan for home fire safety, for example, an assessment point would be her presenting the client with the list of recommended actions that would match the investigation of the client's home setting. A simulation could offer "authentic" assessment feedback by dramatizing in a brief scenario how the application of the plan saves the home from damage (or does not):   this kind of experiential outcome is more involving than scoring the learners' plans against a checklist, for instance.

Presenting a revised story to the editor in the news simulation, or opening the letter from the company interviewer in the negotiating simulation are other examples of assessment points at which feedback from the selected interactions informs learners of their progress toward the simulation's goals. To involve learners more deeply in the assessment experience, we can directly suggest questions for them to reflect upon or provide the option of querying the simulation for guidance with questions they may select before making their decision at such assessment points.

Clearly, these points also offer the chance for learners to ask themselves whether other choices might have produced more satisfactory results or whether there are steps which still need to be taken or other strategies to try. The amount of guidance which the designer provides at these points can vary according to the nature of the learners and the setting of the learning experience.

Keeping track of choices

Often self-instructional material provides a means for learners to record various choices made along the way in order to facilitate the development of appropriate and helpful reflective questions. A "notepad" or "notebook" section for a simulation is a frequently used device. So-called learning logs are like such notebooks, affording a place for learners to record information they want to remember, questions they want to ask, points they may want to investigate further, as well as personal reactions to the experience. Again, the designer can vary the degree of structure available to learners for such notebooks or logs to assist and encourage reflection.

Another recording tool which may help learners construct understanding is the concept frame, a matrix or table in which similar things are analyzed in terms of the presence or absence of certain attributes. An example is shown below. Ongoing entry of information in such a framework affords the learner a means to review his or her understanding, identify areas needing more exploration, and a means to see connections and associations.

	Redwood	Digger Pine	Ponderosa	Incense Cedar	Sugar Pine	Whitebark Pine
Needle foliage		x	x		x	x
Scale foliage	x			x		
Low elevation	x	x				
Middle elevation			x	x	x	
High elevation						x
Economic value	x		x		x	

Concept Frame: Conifers

It is important to remember that assessment points in this format are not quite the same as criterion level questions of the kind we considered with expository lessons. The focus in the experiential style is on the *process* of applying the end competency in increasingly challenging or varying ways rather than upon a pass-no pass criterion of knowledge or skill itself at any given point. Assessment is reflected in monitoring continuous progress, rather than in reaching a single outcome. We are trying to help novices apply knowledge and utilize skills more expertly with every stage of the experience so that the desired competency may transfer and continue to develop in situations outside the learning setting.

Experiential learning and debriefing

A final and interesting point to consider with this delivery style is the research-based contention that individuals engaging in interactive, open-ended self-instructional experiences seem to desire and benefit from an opportunity to share the experience with others who have had the same or similar individual experiences (Romizowski & Grabowski, 1989; Alessi & Trollip, 1991; Croy, Cook & Green, 1993). Not surprisingly, the range of understanding achieved by a the several members of a group may well be more extensive than that arrived at by any single individual within the group, and all can benefit from sharing personal insights. In both school and business training settings, a combination of individual experience with group debriefing has been shown to be a very strong learning combination.

IMPORTANT TO NOTE

Humans are social creatures, and learning is an especially social activity since it is based on communication, the exchange of ideas and information between people. The constructivist view that individuals construct their understanding of the world from their experiences within it clearly includes experiences and interactions with others. The social nature of learning is strongly emphasized by many contemporary psychologists. Such ideas as cognitive apprenticeship clearly reflect the view that considerable human learning arises from novice interacting with expert, from the learner's contact with a more capable other, whether peer or mentor. We should not lose sight of the important fact that "self-instruction" does not mean learning "all by yourself." Our final section will explore the implications of self-directed learning more fully, from both an individual and social point of view.

Representing design-development work

The work of designing and developing simulations is obviously extensive and demanding. Many of us interested in learning about designing self-instruction are more likely to be responsible for planning and carrying out learning experiences rather than designing and producing instructional materials. Often the designers of simulations must communicate the initial planning stages to other team members for actual production. Let's look back at the ideas for flow-charting, script writing and story-boarding, the basic tools of many forms of instructional planning, and see how we may need to adapt them to apply them to laying out the structure of a simulation.

Flow chart variations

We saw earlier that at least two stages of flow chart can be helpful in laying out plans for instruction. A basic diagram of the main content blocks of information is a useful first stage, and a more detailed chart of the flow of information through various decision points and the resulting alternative paths is the second. We will also need to consider, for the more complex multi-layered format we have been considering for simulations, the optional choices which we can offer that not all learners will take.

Recall the notion of a three-dimensional model for progressing through a body of information. We can conceive of these additional levels of information underlying the main layer of information, through which the learner may dig as deeply as he wishes to find answers or assistance, and from which he returns to the basic flow of the simulation. At a simple level, we have various means available to us. The pop-up fields and "hot text" options of such authoring programs as Hypercard or HyperStudio or Tool Book afford a simple one-step jump to another layer and an automatic return. More complex or lengthy choice-option sequences will require more careful planning and clear charting to assure that all learner choices enhance understanding and help develop the intended competency.

For these more extensive optional sequences, a sub-flow chart of the content blocks and interactions can be indicated as "available on interrupt," with a designation to the return and continue from the point where the learner selected the interruption. A rough example of a format for such an optional sequence is shown here.

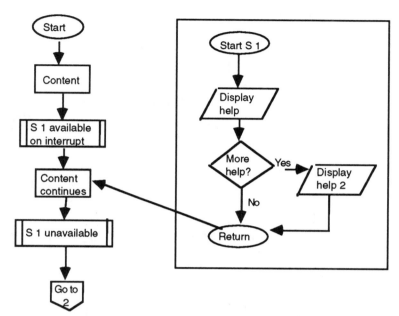

"Available on interrupt" help

The techniques of writing specific instructions to control connections between and among blocks of information are not very difficult to master in many current authoring programs, ranging from tools readily available in schools to more complex materials developed for business and industry. Designers can develop skills in programming and coding content for computer materials using such programs, and may well enjoy the process, but in many organizations designers work teamed with professional programmers skilled in producing the final delivery format to whom they are responsible for communicating a clear basic picture of the desired flow of information.

We have also said that simulations are not limited to computer format: even without coding as an issue, careful organization of possible paths and connections is necessary to assure an effective learning experience. Flow charting is one way to do so.

In summary, to prepare a flowchart,

> Draw a simple flowchart without decision points.
> Add important decisions to create a Level 2 flowchart.
> Create Level 3 flowcharts for more complex material.
> Ensure that decision outcomes and direction of flow are clear and unambiguous.

Scripting

As we discussed in our consideration of developing expository materials, you are now ready to develop the details of content and presentation more fully with a basic script for each of the principal blocks of information. The intended delivery medium for the instruction will obviously dictate the level of detail and the degree of emphasis on visual or text material to be covered in the script. Text to be read by learners requires different qualities than words to be heard by learners: still graphics as illustrations for text require different qualities than video segments of visual information. Because this book is not intended to be specific to any delivery medium we will not delve into techniques for script writing, merely suggest that some kind of overall layout is needed to flesh out your flow chart plan and provide the intermediate guide to the final organization for each component of your material.

Story boarding

Particularly with the complex content of simulations and similar experiential formats, good storyboards can be very helpful. And with the complexities of this kind of material, a sensible and workable coding scheme to identify the type and position of the individual boards is important. These codes can be indicated on your most detailed final flow charts to help with the final development.

Often designers post the storyboards on a wall, or even lay out on the floor the cards or pages they have created, following the flow chart plan, and do an imaginary run through of the various paths that learners might take. Many authors, and the experience of students in my classes, suggest having your peers and colleagues review the story boards from the point of view of instructional designers so that you can revise them before trying a test run with sample members of your potential audience.

Student testing of the material

The completed story boards will provide you with the necessary material for the essential step of student testing of the material, the final core principle for design of self-instruction. The process as described for expository instruction is equally important, and perhaps more so, for inquiry-based materials. You may wish to try out your planned materials in sections to avoid the problems in inter-connections that these more complex materials may turn up. You can at least try to ensure that any one major block of content functions as planned-- options, helps, returns and all-- before finalizing the way that block fits with others. The tryout of the entire sequence will then make it possible to produce the ultimate product of the very extensive and demanding design and development work that goes into creating effective inquiry-based, experiential, simulation kinds of learning experiences.

Summary

Instruction produced in accordance with the philosophy and forms that we have explored in this section can be a very powerful learning experience for learners in a wide range of situations. It would be a mistake, however, to let enthusiasm and interest for the inquiry approach to learning lead us to overlook the original premise of this book: when we are designing *instruction*, we are entering a contract with our learners to afford them the information and experiences that they need to develop the new skills and knowledge that they desire to obtain. To fulfill that contract, the learning experiences we provide must include opportunity to assess the degree of success or the extent of progress toward the desired outcomes.

When we design self-instructional materials and experiences, we are contributing an important component to the wider experience in which each learner is involved, the constructing of his personal knowledge and skill base, and the directing of his personal learning and development. A great deal of learning occurs for all of us throughout our lives without instruction. But those of us in the profession of providing information to learners must be constantly aware of the demands put upon us to do something to that information to make it different, to facilitate learning, to help our learners construct meaning, if we claim to be offering *instruction*.

A look ahead

We opened this book by naming three views of self-directed learning: as a methodology for instruction, as learners' cognitive control processes, and as a philosophy of education. We have looked extensively at this concept as a methodology for developing instructional materials and experiences. Let us now consider some aspects of how individuals may direct and regulate their ongoing learning, to which our self-instructional design materials and methodology may contribute, and some of the issues these considerations raise for the designer of learning experiences. In our final section, we will address the viewpoint of "self-directed learning" as the philosophy of education which underlies the methodology and issues we have discussed in these pages.

REFERENCES AND SUGGESTIONS FOR FURTHER READING

Alessi, S. M., & Trollip, S. R. (1991). Computer-based instruction: Methods and development. (2nd ed.). Englewood Cliffs, NJ: Prentice Hall.

Brown, J. S., Collins, A., & Duguid, P. (1989). Situated cognition and the culture of learning. Educational Researcher, 18,1, 32-42.

Cognition and Technology Group at Vanderbilt. (1990). Anchored instruction and its relationship to situated cognition. Educational Researcher, 19, 6, 2-10.

Collins, A., Brown, J. S., & Newman, S. E. (1989). Cognitive apprenticeship: Teaching the crafts of reading, writing, and mathematics. In L. Resnick (Ed.), Knowing, learning and instruction, (pp. 453-494). Hillsdale, NJ: Erlbaum.

Croy, M. J., Cook, J. R., & Green, M. G. (1993). Human-supplied vs. computer-supplied feedback: an empirical and pragmatic study. Journal of Research on Computing in Education, 26, (2), 185-204.

De Jong, F. P. C. M., & Mensink, J. G. B. (1995). Training cops decisions in deadly force through reflection by use of a powerful learning environment. In Schnase, J. L. & Cunnius, E. L. (Eds.) Proceedings of First International Conference on Computer Support for Collaborative Learning, (pp. 89-93).

Duffy, T. M. & Jonassen, D. H.(Eds). (1992). Constructivism and the technology of instruction: A conversation. Hillsdale, NJ: Erlbaum.

Jonassen, D. H. (1991). Hypertext as instructional design. Educational Technology Research and Development, 39, 83-92.

Jonassen, D. H. (1995). Operationalizing mental models: Strategies for assessing meaningful learning and design-supportive learning environments. In Schnase, J. L. & Cunnius, E. L. (Eds.) Proceedings of First International Conference on Computer Support for Collaborative Learning. (pp. 182-186).

Jones, K. (1987). Simulations: A handbook for teachers and trainers. New York: Nichols.

Keegen, M. Design and effects of scenario educational software. (1993). Educational Technology, June, pp. 19-25.

Kinze, M. B. (1990). Requirements and benefits of effective interactive instruction: Learner control, self-regulation, and continuing motivation. Educational Technology Research & Development, 38, (1), 5-21

McGinn, T. M. (1994). A Constructivist model of instructional design. Unpublished Master's thesis, San Jose State University.

Merrill, M. D. (1988). The Role of tutorial and experiential models in intelligent tutoring systems. Educational Technology, July, pp. 7-13.

O'Neil, H. F., Allred, K., & Baker, E. L. (1992). Measurement of workforce readiness: Review of theoretical frameworks. CSE Technical Report 343, UCLA Center for the Study of Evaluation.

O'Neil, H. F., Allred, K., & Baker, E. L. (1993). Measurement of workforce readiness competencies: Design of prototype measures. CSE Technical Report 344, UCLA Center for the Study of Evaluation.

Paivio, A. (1979). Imagery and verbal processes. Hillsdale, NJ: Erlbaum.

Romiszowski, A. J., & Grabowski, B. (1989). Interactive video and cognitive structures: A technique for enhancing the effectiveness of interactive simulations and games. Paper presented at annual meeting of Association for Educational Communication and Technology, Dallas, TX.

Schanck, R. C., & Cleary, C. (1995). Engines for education. Hillsdale, NJ: Erlbaum.

Schank, R. C., & Jona, M. Y. (1991). Empowering the student: New perspectives on the design of teaching systems. Journal of Learning Sciences, 1, 7-35.

Schank, R. C., Fano, A., Jona, M., & Bell, B. (1993). The design of goal-based scenarios. Technical report #39, Institute for the Learning Sciences, Northwestern University, Evanston, IL.

Thurman, R. A. (1994). Instructional simulation from a cognitive psychology viewpoint. Educational Technology Research and Development, 41, (4), 75-90.

Twitchell, D. (Ed.) (1990). Robert M. Gagne and M. David Merrill: In conversation. Educational Technology, Vol. #, p. 37. (quotation cited) Ref. pp. 35-46.

Van Nostran, W. J. (1989). Scriptwriter's handbook. White Plains, NY: Knowledge Industry Publications.

Willis, J. (1995). A recursive, reflective instructional design model based on constructivist-interpretivist theory. Educational Technology, 35, (6), 5-23.

Wilson, B., & Cole, P. (1992). A review of cognitive teaching models. Educational Technology Research and Development, 39, (4), 47-64.

Yordy, L. (1991). Incorporating learning research into instructional program design. <u>Journal of Educational Technology Systems</u>, <u>19</u> (3), 223-231.

Chapter Four: Issues in "Self-Directed Learning"

In this section of this book let us pause and consider some fundamental issues in learning theory which apply across all delivery styles and which affect all formats for self-instruction. We have looked extensively at "self-directed learning" techniques for designing learning experiences. What do we know about the cognitive strategies which learners employ which are also termed "self-directed learning?" And what are their implications for the learner-centered educational paradigms we encounter today?

Affective issues: motivation, learning styles, interest

To encourage learners' self-direction, we as designers must move into the affective domain, the area of feelings and attitudes as we meet them in learning situations. Gagne names "Attitude" as one of the possible outcomes of instruction. Indeed, how people feel about the topic we teach and their experiences in the learning situation is always an outcome of learning, whether we intend it or not. Issues of motivation, preference for learning style and interest all enter into the attitudes of learners which may either encourage and stimulate self-directed learning, or present obstacles and constraints to learning. How we address our own beliefs about our roles as educators profoundly affects the learning experiences we design. Let us look first at the issue of motivation.

Motivation

We noted at the outset that instruction assumes that learning is the intended outcome of interacting with a body of information. The learner brings to this implied contract his willingness to do the work necessary to reach the desired learning outcome, a willingness we can call "motivation." Motivation is evidenced in learners who make an effort to learn and who show persistence in that effort. We will consider in a moment the possible sources of that motivation and some implications for instructional design inherent in our understanding of motivation.

In many situations, the intent to learn is clearly evident in the simple fact that learners embark upon the interaction: they register for the course, purchase the instructional books or disks, or otherwise obviously signal an intention to learn what the instruction says it offers. We refer to motivation as "intrinsic" when it springs from learners' interest or their perceived need or desire to learn.

Not all instructional settings, however, are voluntary. Sometimes the intention to learn must be stimulated in an audience which is required or expected to learn from an encounter with self-instruction. In an imposed learning situation, motivation arises when learners see the learning as a means to another desired end. This motivation that comes in from the outside, so to speak, is "extrinsic." When learners accept the instruction as important or instrumental to some other goal they seek, the "extrinsic" becomes part of their own choice to learn. Whether intrinsic or extrinsic, the critical element in motivation is the learner's sense of choosing to follow through. The neutral or even reluctant learner poses special challenges to the designer to stimulate motivation to learn, but all learners will benefit from instruction designed to support and encourage the motivation and intent they bring to the learning situation. What do we know about designing instruction that will lead to a positive attitude on the part of our learners?

Keller's ARCS model

John Keller's work exploring motivation to learn is particularly useful to instructional designers who want to make a positive attitude part of the learning experience. This model applies to both school and work learning. Keller names as aspects of motivation

Attention, Relevance, Confidence, and Satisfaction.

<u>Attention</u> This first element in Keller's model can be designed into instruction in many ways. We considered earlier how the layout of material and the choice of wording can affect the communication of information: these factors can be put into service to gain attention as well. Type size and style, color, graphic devices such as arrows, even sound can function as attention-getters. It is easier to develop such perceptual attention-getters

KELLER'S ARCS MODEL
Attention
Relevance
Confidence
Satisfaction

than it is to maintain a tone and style which will hold learners' interest and attention, but it is necessary to try to do both. In general, providing variety, novelty and involvement are important in self-instructional materials, just as they are in other forms of instruction. In fact, the "active responding" aspect of self-instruction helps provide an attention-sustaining atmosphere in itself when properly utilized.

<u>Relevance</u> Making content relevant will draw on our skills in thinking up meaningful and pertinent examples and non-examples for the learners we are working with. The analysis of the intended audience which precedes all good design efforts should provide background information to help with this effort.

Learners will also relate their learning activities to the desired outcomes and maintain motivation when they clearly understand objectives at the outset. This does not necessarily imply that you must present a list of formally stated "you will be able to" outcomes in your introduction, but it does suggest that you provide a clear description of the nature and purpose of the instruction as you begin.

Confidence Confidence arises from experiencing success as learners progress through instruction, yet we need to keep interactions sufficiently challenging for the feeling of success to be significant. If we have been working on developing material which requires appropriately thoughtful responding, challenge should be a built-in aspect. The principles of small steps, self-pacing and immediate feedback can help us provide these confidence-building success experiences also, through keeping blocks of content a manageable size, dealt with at a pace which is controlled by the learners, and by offering remediation and help to assure that they attain success. Immediate feedback means that learners always have a good idea of where they are and how they are progressing, which fosters confidence.

Satisfaction The manner in which feedback is provided can also enhance satisfaction in self-instruction. Since the usual self-instructional situation does not include teachers or peers, it is important to remember to include in our design of materials the appropriate acknowledgment of the attainment of goals or mile

---

APPLYING THE ARCS MODEL TO AN INTRODUCTORY PASSAGE
FOR SELF-INSTRUCTIONAL MATERIAL

ATTENTION:
Because you bought this study program booklet, you identify yourself as one of more than 200 practitioners who plan to take the XX recertification exam this spring. Will you pass it?

RELEVANCE:
Being an effective XX requires that you not only remember what you learned about your profession in school, but also that you've stayed current with the field. Some of the study material for the exam in this booklet reviews basics: some will ask questions about the newer developments in XX which you have met in workshops, reading, or on-the-job training.

CONFIDENCE:
References providing necessary information about the newest aspects are included in this booklet. Study these references before taking the sample exam, and again after taking it to review what you missed. Each year applicants taking the recertification exam tell us that they scored solid "pass" grades by studying this review program. You can too.

SATISFACTION:
Passing the exam means more than scoring well on a test: you have the satisfaction of knowing that you are a professional, up-to-date XX, able to serve the public effectively in your chosen work. Good luck!

---

stones. Good design can help to provide the sense of satisfaction which motivates learners to continue to work as necessary toward the final satisfaction of evaluating their learning against the intent which they brought to the experience.

While the ARCS model suggests a sequence of steps in designing motivational instruction, all four elements can be woven into any given single segment of instruction. See the example in the box to illustrate a conscious effort to address them all in an introductory passage. You will benefit from keeping all these elements in mind as you work on all the various sections of your content material.

(As a footnote to the ARCS model, it is interesting to note that Keller's original list of motivational elements was "Interest, Relevance, Expectancy, and Satisfaction." (Keller, in Reigeluth, 1983.) The change to the ARCS list is seen in a 1987 article. I can't think of a better illustration of the effect of form upon communicating an idea and prompting its recall by association. "IRES" just doesn't make it: the carefully crafted shift to "ARCS" is all the difference.)

Attribution research

An aspect of both the confidence and satisfaction that Keller names as motivational is the question of what learners believe are the reasons for a successful and satisfying learning experience. "Attribution theory" is the study of people's beliefs about their learning, and it has a lot to tell us about the design of instruction, especially about feedback.

Success by itself is not enough to provide satisfaction with the learning experience. If a learner believes he succeeded at a task because he invested the necessary effort and stuck to it, he has one kind of feeling about that success. A very different feeling results about the success if he feels the task was boringly simple, or that succeeding was just a lucky guess. Similarly, failing can be overcome and even contribute usefully to learning, if a learner believes she failed due to quitting too soon or not trying quite hard enough, not because the task was too difficult or she just doesn't have the ability required, or "This was not my lucky day."

The term used in the literature for how hard people think a task will be is the "perceived demand characteristic" of the task. A second term relating to this issue is "perceived self-efficacy," which is the learner's belief about his or her ability to accomplish the task. (You sometimes see these referred by their initials: PDC and PSE.) Note that both aspects are identified in terms of learner perception: as designers, we can affect the perception of both task difficulty and personal ability to accomplish it by the way we structure the interactions with content which we offer to learners. We can simplify difficult tasks for beginners, and we can set up more challenging interactions for experienced learners. It is even possible with some technological delivery settings to let learners identify themselves as new or experienced and allow that choice to govern the format of the material they will work on.

One more term may be useful here. Gavriel Salomon (1984) uses the term "Amount of Invested Mental Effort" to describe how involved learners become with the learning experience. Making instruction engaging by applying what we know from motivation research can be the designer's contribution to the investment of the necessary mental effort. Look back over some of the techniques we discussed in the preceding sections in the light of this research.

<u>Feedback Issues in Attribution Research</u> The power of learners' attributions makes it important for designers to think carefully about the form of feedback for both successes and failures. "Positive reinforcement" for success has to help the learner feel reinforced for contributing the effort and persistence that led to the success. Telling a child, "Good job!" is more effective than saying, "You are so smart!" Learners who become accustomed to attributing success to ability may have major problems when facing inevitable failures. It is not uncommon to find bright children who are "unmotivated." Perhaps they are really strongly motivated, motivated to avoid failing in order to defend their picture of themselves. "I could do it if I wanted to: I just don't want to." Good self-directed learning experiences, with a series of small step successes, can help such learners to regain confidence and curiosity and begin to attribute desired outcomes to the qualities which they can control, not only to a particular innate ability.

Saying "Good job, but..." when the learner himself knows or suspects that the job is *not* very good is even less effective. Straightforward information is the best feedback rather than the mixed message of such qualified statements of praise. Providing further information, or opportunities for assistance or for alternate actions will encourage learners to try again or to try another strategy,

and improves their chances for the investment of appropriate amounts of mental effort
and for appropriate attributions.

A review of research on this issue notes that
"evidence converges on one point: success or
failure itself may be less important than an individual's perception of the causes of the success or failure." (Stipek and Wiesz, 1981).
Ensuring success experiences is important, but
the relationship between what learners do and
their level of success must be clear to them.
The active responding and immediate feedback of self-instruction can help learners to
accept responsibility for their successes, and to
experience the rewards of persistence and
effort to overcome failure.

Androgogy and pedagogy

A great deal of recent research on self-directed
learning addresses adult learners. The work of
Malcolm Knowles has been especially important in calling attention to the special learning
needs of adults. The term "andragogy" describes the field of teaching adults as it is con-
trasted with "pedagogy," the teaching of children. The table summarizes some principal
distinctions often named as indicative of the
differences between the way children and
adults learn.

While it is clear that children do in fact have
less life experience than grown-ups, and it is

DIFFERENCES BETWEEN ADULTS AND CHILDREN	
Adult Characteristics	Children's Characteristics
Autonomy	Dependence
Active role as learners	Receptive role as learners
Life experience as a resource	Little experience to draw on
Need to relate learning to present life situation	Learning for future use
Responsible for their own learning	Teacher is responsible

also true that much school learning lays a foundation for future rather than immediate use, I think it is a mistake to consider children as receptive and dependent to the degree here suggested. Children of course rely on adults to provide the context and support for their learning, but this does not mean that they must depend on adults to control their learning. Of course teachers are responsible for providing many more aspects of the learning situation for children than for adult students, but if we lose sight of children's self-directedness, we seriously inhibit their learning potential.

Interesting studies by various researchers (e.g. Deci, 1992; Pressley et al. 1992) show quite conclusively that children may lose interest and motivation in learning when they are either pressured or even directly rewarded for certain performances. Pressures and rewards that children experience as controlling reduce their curiosity and willingness to accept challenge. However, learning settings which preserve and encourage children's sense of autonomy, of willingly choosing to do something, increase not only their motivation but their learning. This is not to suggest that children do only what they want to do in school: it does, however, strongly suggest providing a context which encourages a sense of competence and which helps children relate content to be learned to what is interesting and meaningful to them.

In DeCharms' studies of motivation with inner-city children, (e.g. 1968) he uses two terms which powerfully sum up children's perceptions of their learning experiences. He describes his subjects as seeing themselves as "origins or pawns." One of the greatest potential benefits of good self-instructional situations for both children and adults is the possibility of providing learning experiences in which the learners function as "origins," the source and controlling element in their learning, rather than as pawns manipulated by others.

Engagement and games

Given the convincing research evidence for the power of motivational instruction, how can we develop materials that incorporate Keller's elements, build on all this work, and produce the sense of "origin" for our learners?

We can get another set of helpful ideas from the work of Malone, whose early work investigated what made computer games so

MALONE'S ELEMENTS OF ENGAGEMENT
Challenge 　　Curiosity 　　　　Fantasy 　　　　　　Control

engrossing, especially for children. He identified the elements of challenge, curiosity, and fantasy as critical components of the observable engagement of players with computer games. His later work extended these observations to computer based instruction as well as games, and he and his co-worker, Lepper, added the element of control to the former list.

We have already considered the aspect of challenge, of providing enough difficulty in a lesson without making goals too hard to reach as we considered Keller's element of satisfaction above. Similarly, Malone's "curiosity" is quite parallel to Keller's "attention." Like Keller, Lepper and Malone (1987) note that instruction must go beyond affording the sensory surprises which attract attention, to providing learning situations with information which learners see as possibly contradictory, incomplete or unexpected to stimulate them to seek new information to resolve the conflict.

Confidence and control are also similar, and we have discussed each at length above. "Learner control" does not mean that students make all the decisions about the instruction: research has shown that students frequently do not make good choices about the direction of a lesson (e.g., Carrier, 1984). Malone emphasizes that the sense of control arises when student choices lead to outcomes directly and clearly related to the student's action. The result does not even have to be a desired outcome: the important point here is that the result is clearly contingent upon the learner's action. Thus the "control" of either success or failure remains attributable to the learner's choice of action. Such perceived control keeps learners committed and involved, functioning as DeCharms' "origins" of the learning experience. Autonomy for the learner is essential to the establishing of a true "implied contract" for all instruction, not only self-instruction, but it is critical for true self-directed learning.

Fantasy is an interesting element in Malone's list, a very obvious component of many of the games he investigated. Imagining oneself in exciting and dramatic contexts is fun, as Malone noted in observing the game players engrossed in being treasure hunters, space ship pilots, jungle adventurers. Incorporating fantasy into instruction need not, however, require spaceships or time travel: designers can incorporate all kinds of scenarios to give context to lesson content in tutorials as well as games, drills or simulations. Exploring how to manage a classroom, run a business, calculate scientific reactions are examples of such simulation formats, all of which provide the strongly motivational effect of letting learners ask questions and take chances which have no real-world consequences. Envisioning a situation in which you would really use what you are learning is a great help to learning it. (Designing and developing such learning experiences for self-instruction can be fun for the designer too, and we may need to remind ourselves that the outcomes of instruction have to be real, regardless of its imagined contexts. We have to hold up our end of the contract.)

Learning style variations and preferences

People learn in many different ways. Howard Gardner has recently proposed seven different "intelligences," broad organizational structures in which given groups of people seem to function most effectively as learners. Throughout history, since Hippocrates time, we have recognized that people vary in temperament. Many kinds of categorizations for personality and learning style preferences have been developed by various researchers.

Interestingly, most such classifications, like Hippocrates temperaments, group people into four main groups with assorted combinations determining characteristics which may affect their learning. Some references to the work in this area are included at the end of this section but we will content ourselves at this point with considering the observable learner preferences which probably affect design of self-instruction most significantly.

"Learning style" as a term describes an individual's consistent patterns of perception and processing of new information. Some of these characteristics are probably inborn and some result from development and experience. A strong point about self-instruction is the extent to which it affords learners the opportunity to learn as they prefer.

One broad, basic division for learning styles identifies three principal learning "modalities:" auditory, visual, and kinesthetic. (Preference for tactile or manipulative learning experiences is sometimes separated out from the broader kinesthetic modality.) Researchers such as Keefe (1979) and Dunn and Dunn (1979) suggest that perhaps 20 to 30 percent of us learn new information best through auditory channels, some 40 percent of us are visual, and perhaps 30 to 40 per cent are kinesthetic learners or a combination of these three modalities.

With the current development of multi-media formats as options for presenting lesson information, the question of learner preference takes on particular interest. The implications are clear for providing learner-selected options for sound, graphics, text and even manipulation of elements of the presented material as a means of accommodating learning style and modality preference.

People also differ very basically in their cognitive processing style. For a number of years we used the terms "left brain" and "right brain" to describe the difference between people with a verbal, sequential, analytic style of information processing in contrast to people who tend to employ global, holistic, more spatial reasoning patterns. There is some real evidence for hemisphere difference, but whatever the biological basis, the difference in emphasis upon sequence is evident in learner preferences. Again, the opportunity is present in designing self-instructional material for providing learners with appropriate options for the order in which they proceed through some kinds of content and for extending their overall view of a topic through branching and linking choices.

Learners differ as well in their preference for structure and their tolerance for uncertainty. Once again, many of the options available to the designer of self-instructional material can help address these preferences: various levels of help may be provided, alternate paths through instructional material may be offered, and with some kinds of computer-based instruction, a record of learner choices can be kept and automatic guidance or advisement can be triggered.

Whatever delivery medium you work with, awareness of the variety of learning styles which your learners may possess can help you make effective decisions about your presentation of information, the guidance and practice you provide, and the kinds of assessment you offer in the instruction which you design.

STIMULI	ELEMENTS	
Environmental	Sound Temperature	Light Design of room
Emotional	Motivation Responsibility	Persistence Degree of structure preferred
Sociological	Self Peers, team	Pairs Degree of management
Physical	Perceptual Time	Nourishment intake Mobility
Psychological	Hermisphericity Impulsivity vs. reflectiveness Global vs. analytic processing style	

Aspects of Learning Styles

Learning Styles: Dunn and Dunn

A final consideration about learning style preference is found in the work of Rita and Kenneth Dunn, who proposed a set of five classes of stimuli governing a range of learner preferences. They named as considerations environmental, emotional, sociological, physical and psychological elements of a learning situation. We have considered above several aspects included in the emotional and psychological elements of their model.

Many of the elements of environmental and physical stimuli and preferences are beyond the control of the designer of self-instructional material. Some delivery systems do permit adjustment of sound level, brightness and so on which may be presented as choices to learners to help match their preferences. Our observance of the principle of self-pacing will allow learners to take breaks, move around or similarly adapt their preferences and needs to the self-instructional learning setting, at least to some degree.

As we have repeatedly emphasized, the careful analysis of the potential learning audience is essential for the design of all instruction. Learning preferences and needs affected by cultural and sociological factors must be addressed as we start a design project.

We will return to give some consideration to the sociological setting and people's preferences for working alone or with others as we consider collaborative formats for self-instruction. Generally, self-instruction carries with it the suggestion that an individual learner is provided with as wide a range of possible matches for learning style preference as can be devised: this potential for a match between learner needs and instructional format is frequently named as one of the great strengths of self-instruction.

Interest

As an umbrella concept, interest offers us a convenient term to apply to our designs for self-instruction. We want our materials to be interesting: in common usage, this suggests that people will be motivated to learn by working with those materials, and that there is a match between their personal learning styles and the materials which they find engaging and stimulating, in short, interesting.

When people say they are interested in something, there is a strong element of curiosity implied. Think of how often you have heard people comment when presented with a piece of information: "That's interesting. What....?" or "That's interesting. How.....?" or "...Where?" Questions seem to arise naturally from interest.

Seeking answers to our questions is at the core of learning new information. As we have seen, frequently learners bring this readiness to a self-instructional setting and we find them already interested and motivated to learn. Obviously, one of the most powerful means at our command for encouraging learning is responding to or stimulating this questioning response in our learners. The strong tie between interest as a state of mind and question-asking as a behavior can be very effectively turned to our advantage as designers of self-instruction.

There is an intriguing body of literature investigating the effect of "adjunct questions" in text. This simply means the effect of posing questions as people read through a passage. Not surprisingly, material about which questions are asked tends to be remembered and subsequently recalled at a significantly higher level.

Research has also established that when questions are asked *before* text is presented, readers tend to focus their attention on and recall the material related to those questions to the exclusion of other information. When a series of questions is asked only after a passage of text is read, readers often cannot readily recall the material being asked about. Interspersing questions throughout a passage had the maximum effect upon learning and recall in many of these studies (Rothkopf & Bisbicos, 1967; Anderson, 1975; Reynolds & Anderson, 1982; E. Gagne, 1985).

(We should note that these studies did not necessarily show that learners found the material interesting, merely that they recognized it as important and paid attention to it. Further, these studies focus on reading, and we are in this book considering a wider range of information-presentation formats. What is significant for our purposes at this point is the relationship between questioning and learning.)

Guiding our thinking: Meta-cognition

As people learn, modify their schemas, aim at their cognitive objectives, there is a layer of skills that direct their thinking which are usually referred to as <u>meta</u> cognitive skills, from the Greek word that signifies "with," "above," or "in common with." These are the management skills that help people think about their thinking. They accompany and mesh with the strategies and techniques of direct interaction with content which learners employ. Such self-regulating activities during learning, as they have been studied by many researchers, are seen to arise from reflective thinking, an aspect of learning which has been discussed since John Dewey's work.

Reflection refers to the purposeful pause in the thinking process which occurs when a person consciously stops to assess or question the procedure he is following in dealing with the information or problem he is working with. Clearly, more is involved than simply stopping to chew the end of the pencil and puzzle about what to do next. True reflection has the effect of stepping back from immediate involvement to try to obtain a bigger picture of the situation. Reflection during learning seems to be an observable trait in successful learners: encouraging such reflection for all learners can be a component of well-designed instructional materials and activities.

Meta-cognitive skills

Broadly speaking, reflective self-regulation appears both in the planning stages of a learning situation and also in the ongoing monitoring of actions taken during learning. Good learners have probably developed most of these skills unconsciously through ongoing experiences of successful learning. Let's consider what good learners may automatically do which we could encourage our learners to do by the way we design and present our materials. Current research identifies five aspects of such self-regulation or meta-cognitive activity:

Planning	Deciding direction of learning activities
Selecting	Determining important information
Connecting	Relating new information to known information
Tuning	Trying out, practicing, adjusting new information
Monitoring	Checking progress, assessing results

These kinds of meta-cognitive activity are what keep learners engaged in the process of learning, allowing them to work with the information at hand to promote their own particular learning.

The view of instruction as the "implied contract" we have talked about earlier suggests that good design should offer help to learners in getting to the right level of managing the learning experience. By affording choice, we may guide without insisting, making help available to those needing it and getting out of the way of those not needing it. We can, for example, try to do some of the initial organizing for learners and then let them build on a base that matches their level of need. We can provide appropriate emphasis in our choice of wording or visuals to encourage effective se-

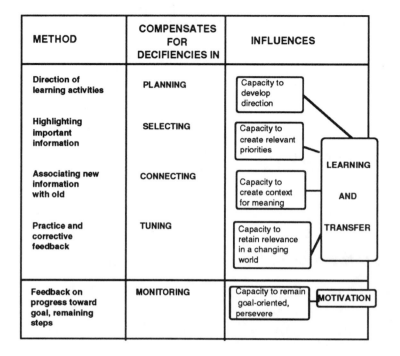

lecting, and provide enough variety in examples and activities to make connecting more likely for our learners. The kinds of practice and experiences which we provide for interaction with content concepts and procedures can influence the learners' tuning and monitoring processes

We can see that the idea of scaffolding discussed earlier reflects not only provision of necessary information content to meet learners' needs, but the provision of opportunities and choices to assist the process of learning. For novice learners, the accompanying diagram suggests ways in which we may design the learning experience to compensate for lack of developed skill. However, a major point to remember in considering the effect of meta-cognition on learning is that our intent is to help foster learners' internalization of these skills, not to substitute for them. Here is another important reason for trying to design adaptive, experiential learning approaches.

Summary

While learning involves cognition and the acquiring of both declarative and procedural knowledge, major influences on the success or failure of learning opportunities lie in the attitudes and feelings of learners toward the experience. As designers, we can help further successes and avoid failures for our learners by addressing the issues considered here.

A look ahead

In our final section let us return to the third understanding of "self-directed learning" named at the beginning of this book, the view that a belief in "self-directed learning" constitutes an important philosophy of education, one increasingly addressed in the educational paradigms which we work with in today's world of rapid change, new learning needs, and new processes and resources for the instructional designer.

REFERENCES AND SUGGESTIONS FOR FURTHER READING

Carrier, C. (1984). Do learners make good choices? Instructional Innovator, 29 (2), 15-17.

Corno, L., & Mandinach, E. B. (1983). Role of cognitive engagement in classroom learning and motivation. Educational Psychologist, 18 (2), 88-108.

DeCharms, R. (1968). Personal causation. New York: Academic Press.

Deci, E. L. (1992). The relation of interest to the motivation of behavior: A self-determination theory perspective. In Renninger, K. A., Hidi, S, & Krapp, A. (Eds.) The role of interest in learning and development. Hillsdale, NJ: Erlbaum, pp. 43-70.

Dunn, R., & Dunn, K. (1978). Teaching students through their individual learning styles: A practical approach. New York: Reston.

Dunn, R. S., Dunn, K. J., & Price, G. E. (1979). Identifying individual learning styles. In National Association of Secondary School Principals, Student learning styles: Diagnosing and prescribing programs. Reston, VA: National Association of Secondary School Principals.

Gardner, H. (1983). Frames of mind. New York: Basic Books.

Keefe, J. W. (Ed.). (1979). Student learning styles: Diagnosing and prescribing programs. Reston, VA: National Association of Secondary School Principals.

Keller, J. M. (1983). Motivational design of instruction. In Reigeluth, C. M., (Ed.) Instructional design theories and models. Hillsdale, NJ: Erlbaum.

Keller, J. M. (1987). Strategies for stimulating the motivation to learn. Performance and Instruction, Vol. , 1-7.

Knowles, M. S. (1980). Modern practice of adult education. (Rev. ed.) Chicago: Association Press.

Malone, T. W. (1981). Towards a theory of intrinsically motivating instruction. Cognitive Science, 5, 333-369.

Malone, T. W., & Lepper, M. R. (1987). Making learning fun: A taxonomy of intrinsic motivations for learning. In Snow, R. E. & Farr, M. J. (Eds.) Aptitude, Learning and Instruction: III Conative and Affective Process Analysis. Hillsdale, NJ: Erlbaum.

Pressley, M., El-Dinary, P. B., Marks, M. B., Brown, R., & Stein, S. (1992). Good strategy instruction is motivating and interesting. In Renninger, K. A., Hidi, S., & Krapp, A. (Eds.) The role of interest in learning and development. Hillsdale, NJ: Erlbaum, pp. 333-358.

Reynolds, R. E., & Anderson, R. C. (1982). Influence of questions on the allocation of attention during reading. Journal of Educational Psychology, 74, 623-632.

Rothkopf, E. Z., & Bisbicos, E. E. (1967). Selective facilitative effects of interspersed questions on learning from written material. Journal of Educational Psychology, 58, 56-61.

Salamon, G. (1984). Television is "easy" and print is "tough:" Differential investment of mental effort in learning as a function of perceptions and attributions. Journal of Educational Psychology, 76 ,(4), 647-658.

Sagerman, N., & Mayer, R. E. (1987). Forward transfer of different reading strategies evoked by adjunct questions in science text. <u>Journal of Educational Psychology</u>, <u>79</u> ,(2), 189-191.

Walters, J. M., & Gardner, H. (1988). The theory of multiple intelligences: Some issues and answers. In Sternberg, R. J., & Wagner, R. K. (Eds.) <u>Practical intelligence</u>. New York: Cambridge University Press.

Chapter Five: Self-directed Learning, A Final Look

We began our consideration of self-directed learning by noting that there are several possible understandings of the idea of self-directed learning. We have explored the concept at length under its definition as a format for the delivery of instruction to individual learners, considering both expository and inquiry approaches to such instruction, and further as the set of skills and abilities which individuals employ to guide their cognitive experiences in learning situations. The fullest understanding of the term moves us into consideration of what we ourselves believe and attempt to practice as educators and designers, our philosophy of education, our convictions about the appropriate relationship between seekers of knowledge and those of us whose profession it is to attempt to help people in that search.

Self-directed Learning in Collaborative Settings

We have spent a major part of this book looking at self-instruction from the point of view of designing learning materials for individual learners, probably the most common perspective on the idea of "self-directed learning." However, we have already noted that working with such materials is not necessarily an all-alone activity but one which may fruitfully combine others in pairs or small groups. We have also noted that individual learning activity frequently benefits from and may even need a group debrief experience to bring it to a conclusion (e.g. Romizowski & Grabowski, 1989). Review of one's work, as we have seen, is an effective learning strategy.

Designing learning experiences

We can expand on this view by considering how the design of self-directed learning really implies the design of the learning experience rather than simply the learning materials. "Collaborative learning" is a more precise description than is "cooperative learning" of the learning experience we are considering, as it emphasizes the mutual engagement of learners in solving a problem rather than the division of labor to reach a group goal, though both terms may be found in the literature on small group learning. Further, "collaborative" may better acknowledge the role of the teacher or designer in such experiences.

Small Group Learning Settings

Small group learning settings have received considerable research investigation in recent years. From our point of view, one very obvious but not always stated aspect of designing successful small group work is that the skills and behaviors necessary for effective group work should be taught to learners as preparation for such experiences. Thus, designing for the more self-directed learning experiences which small group work can foster clearly requires consideration in the "providing information" stage of including for any given group the concepts and skills that they need to know for successful interaction.

Younger students in particular benefit from initial guidance in group learning activities, which are more student-directed than teacher-directed. However, older learners, who may be accustomed to some degree of individual and personal direction of their learning, may also work better with others when particular skills or techniques are formally designed into the learning situation. Numerous team-building activities are described in the literature, not only for school settings but increasingly for adult learners in business and industry. To present such approaches in detail is beyond the scope of this work, but readers are directed to the references by Cohen, Davidson, Scholtes and others in the bibliography as representative of useful techniques and formats for such introductory experiences.

The main point to be aware of in the design of effective group self-instructional experiences, just as in the design of effective individual self-instructional experiences, is that the role of both teacher and learner is differently focused. It is fairly easy to see the change in the role of teacher from the actions and ideas which govern a good expository style: the change in the role of the students, however, is even more critical and should be directly addressed by the design of the learning experience. Learners must move from being receivers of information to becoming active investigators, from answering questions to generating them.

Note that these changes apply also to instructional settings other than classrooms with live instructors. Computer-based systems are currently being developed which employ the "coaching" model for the computer's role and which require of the learners, either individually or collaboratively, questioning, critiquing and assessing actions rather than simply receiving and applying information (Katz & Lesgold, 1993; de Jong & Mensik, 1995; Gibbons, Fairweather, Anderson & Merrill, 1996).

A growing body of research worldwide is appearing from the work of investigators interested in collaborative learning experiences both in educational settings and in the workplace. Much of the work in this area reflects a parallel interest in the incorporation of computer support for such learning. (CSCL

Proceedings, 1995). The rapid development of networked computing and the implications of the Internet and the World Wide Web for learning raise many issues and questions for designers. However, as Kaptelenin (1995) has aptly observed, to be of true value, the emphasis of research must be on the interaction of the learning experience with the computer tools rather than on devising learning experiences to make use of the available tools.

Co-Design as a concept for today

Finally, we should look at current considerations of what may be seen as perhaps the ultimate stage of designing collaborative learning experiences: when groups themselves address the issues we have discussed to design and develop learning experiences. The "learning organization" as seen by Senge (1990) represents this concept, though frequently a designer/consultant, like the designer/teacher in more formal educational settings, may be an important catalyst.

Involving those who will do the work of learning in the framing of the questions to be asked and answered grows out of the concerns we have identified in inquiry-based learning. Yet clearly, seekers of knowledge often do not know exactly what question they in fact wish to ask, and it remains a responsibility of the designer-partner to afford guidance and assistance in this endeavor. This approach resembles "needs analysis" but reflects the different viewpoint which newer paradigms embrace (Willis, 1995). Work done in this area has grown in part out of concerns for computer-human interface design, with a logical extension from the concerns of users of technology as working tools to the concerns of these users with technology as cognitive tools (e.g. Schuler & Namioka, 1993).

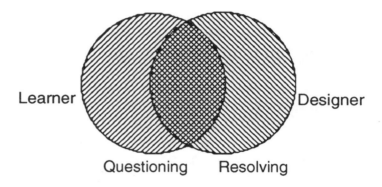

Aspects of Co-Design

My personal experience with this design approach began with the collaborative design of an ongoing program for the training of consultants and/or entrepreneurs through the Instituto Technologico de Monterrey in Mexico starting in 1994 (Davila & Keirns, 1994). Working with this program continues to develop my conviction that optimum learning occurs when learners and designers form a partnering relationship throughout the learning experience, as managers of "learning organizations" must do in the world of business.

Not only in business and industry settings do we find "learning organizations" developing. In forward-looking schools today, teachers and researchers are establishing settings which expect students to learn how to pose as well as how to solve problems and to combine their developing understanding with the insights of others to develop as well as to strive toward learning goals.

As we move into "distributed" or "distance" or "online" learning environments, the changed roles of learner-designer are even more evident. The interface between peers, content, and the directing element of formal courses in these formats alters dramatically and must draw on the learners' input in new ways. We are still exploring these interactions and have much to learn. Some of the ideas we have considered together in this book may well prove useful in such explorations of new partnerships.

Information management and co-design

Changing technology provides some different ways to develop this partnership and requires new skills on the part of the designer. A major current professional skill must be described as information management. Excellent current examples of information management can be found in many museum-type institutions.

Visitors to such places ordinarily bring in the necessary element of "desire to learn" to trigger the opportunity for the designer to partner in the development of the learning situation. Because visiting a museum is usually a self-directed activity, the role of the designer as information manager can be critical to the establishment and fulfillment of a learning experience.

Technology is increasingly a powerful tool in this endeavor. Beyond such basic application of technology as user-controlled audio or CD guided tours, one may find such extensive resources as the Micro Gallery Project at the National Gallery, London, England. This interactive material is far more than a guide or display, and while not directly identifying itself as instruction, affords the user-learner the opportunity to self-determine all of the elements of the constructivist model we considered earlier to build a wealth of learning experiences. Going far beyond the organization of a visual and information data base of the gallery's huge collection, the paths and links afforded the user through this material represent a partnership in information access that is truly a vehicle for the co-design of learning.

The huge information resources of the Internet and the World Wide Web cry out for similar information management if the widely touted access to information is to benefit those hoping to learn from it. Identifying and organizing existing information must parallel the ability to develop and present new bodies of information as a component of the designer-partner's contribution to learning. In addition, the developing conventions of Web page design must increasingly build on our developing understanding not only of learning theory but of the issues in human-computer interface design to reflect our consideration in this arena of what might be termed "cognitive ergonomics."

Vygotsky noted long ago that novice learners reach beyond their current levels of capability in the presence of a "more competent other." Sometimes the teacher-designer is directly in contact with the learner to co-design the paths through information, and act directly as the "more competent other." Perhaps the very nature of the organization of available information by a competent designer can help the information itself function in this role for the self-directed learner.

Self-directed learning as a philosophy of education

The final definition for self-directed learning that we proposed in the opening of this book was that of a philosophy of education. A recognized purpose of education and schooling in every society is to hand on valued knowledge and skills to a new generation. Both research and effective practice suggest that engaging learners' native curiosity is the surest method to establish the lines of communication necessary to reach that goal. Educators who see their role as encouraging and assisting learners to take responsibility for their own learning are committed to this view.

In the provision of information in any content area, a good teacher/designer can afford opportunity for the natural questioning response which we have seen accompanies interest and curiosity. Establishing information-rich educational environments that provide learners the experience of building their knowledge demands considerable effort and preparation of content and activities by teachers and designers. However, whether the work is invested for individual or group experiences, the rewards are many.

The most significant outcome of learning in such settings is not limited to the specific content and skills acquired but lies in the cast of mind fostered by this kind of experience. The habit of generating questions and exploring solutions leads to true self-directed learning as an ongoing and characteristic activity that can be fostered in individuals and groups through the effective learning experiences that result from application of good design and development principles to instructional settings.

Further, in our society today it is becoming an increasingly important goal of education to try to develop learners who will continue to learn and explore an ever-changing world. The world of work expects that people will bring to their jobs a capacity to learn new ideas, to look for better ways to set and achieve goals. Accordingly, a major area for the profession of instructional design is in business and industry. Here, too, the philosophy of education which supports and encourages self-directed learning is more and more appropriate.

Summary

Designers who commit to their roles as partners in a learning experience can best fulfill the implied contract of helping learners both identify and reach desired goals. In order to fruitfully apply this philosophy of education, we must continually hone our own skills and knowledge. We must direct our own learning to seek new ways in which we can design learning experiences that truly do interact with the information we work with to make it different, to facilitate learning.

REFERENCES AND SUGGESTIONS FOR FURTHER READING

Cohen, E. (1986). Designing groupwork. New York: Teachers' College Press.

Davidson, N., & Worsham, T., Eds. (1992). Enhancing thinking through cooperative learning. New York: Teachers' College Press.

Duffy, T. M. & Jonassen, D. H.(Eds). (1992). Constructivism and the technology of instruction. Hillsdale, NJ: Erlbaum.

Gibbons, A. , Fairweather, P. , Anderson, T. , & Merrill, M. D. (1996) Simulation and computer-based instruction: A future view. In press.

Hertz-Lazarowitz, R., & Miller, N. , Eds. (1992). Interaction in cooperative groups. Cambridge: Cambridge University Press.

Katz, S., & Lesgold, A. (1993). The role of the tutor in computer-based collaborative learning situations. In Lajoie, S. P., & Derry, S. J. (Eds.) Computers as cognitive tools. Hillsdale, NJ: Erlbaum.

Koschmann, T., Ed. (1996). CSCL:Theory and practice of an emerging paradigm. Mahwah, NJ: Erlbaum.

Lajoie, S. P., & Derry, S. J., Eds. (1993). Computers as cognitive tools. Hillsdale, NJ: Erlbaum.

Regian, J. W. & Shute, V. J. (eds.) (1992). Cognitive approaches to automated instruction. Englewood Cliffs, NJ: Erlbaum.

Romomiszowski, A. J., & Grabowski, B. (1989). Interactive video and cognitive structures: A technique for enhancing the effectiveness of interactive simulations and games. Paper presented at annual meeting of AECT, Dallas, TX.

Schnase, J. L. & Cunnius, E. L. (Eds.) (1995). Proceedings of First International Conference on Computer Support for Collaborative Learning.

Scholtes, P. R. (1988). The team handbook. Madison, WI: Joiner.

Schuler, D. & Namioka, A. (Eds.) (1993). Participatory design: Principles and practices. Hillsdale, NJ.: Erlbaum.

Senge, P. M. (1990). The fifth discipline: the art and practice of the learning organization. New York: Doubleday.

Sterman, N.,. & Brockenbrough, S. (1991). The mediated museum: Computer-based technology and museum infrastructure. Journal of Educational Technology Systems, 19, (1)

Willis, J. (1995). A recursive, reflective instructional design model based on constructivist-interpretivist theory. Educational Technology, 35, (6), 5-23.

Wilson, B., & Cole, P. (1992). A review of cognitive teaching models. <u>Educational Technology Research and Development</u>, 39, (4), 47-64.

Index of Principal Points

Assessment
9, 45, 47, 49, 87, 92, 93, 108, 109, 114, 115, 117

Collaborative learning
49, 160, 162, 163, 164

Flow charts
68-70, 119-123

Help interactions
3, 5, 109-112, 121, 124, 147

Implied contract of instruction
5, 35-36, 44-45, 48, 76, 90, 93, 113, 132, 144,
153, 169

Planning of instruction
14, 31, 36-37, 68, 70-71, 87-88, 94, 99, 119-120
    Planning Pyramid   41-45, 63
    Planning, meta-cognition 152-153

Principles of self-instruction
9, 28, 67, 73, 100
    Active responding   10, 28, 30, 50, 51,
    53, 56, 61, 63, 67, 73, 100, 134, 140
    Immediate feedback   10, 28, 30, 46, 61,
    73, 86, 100, 135, 140
    Small steps   10, 28, 30, 35, 50,
    51, 61, 63, 71, 73, 112, 135
    Self-pacing   10, 28, 73, 111,
    135, 149
    Testing by students   28, 72-73, 124

Questioning as a learning activity
16-18, 24, 31, 34, 35, 49, 76, 85, 92, 100, 101,
107, 115, 116, 144, 150-151, 162-163, 167-168

Index

Reflection
92, 101, 114-116, 148, 152

Scaffolding
96, 98, 101, 109, 110, 111, 112, 154

Schema
82-83, 89, 90, 91, 151

Story boards
71-72, 123